volume **IV**

NEAR DEATH EXPERIENCES

COMPILED BY LEE NELSON & RICHARD NELSON

N.D.E. volume IV

NEAR DEATH
EXPERIENCES

ISBN: 1-55517-366-7

Published and Distributed by:

925 North Main, Springville, UT 84663 • 801/489-4084

CFI Publishing and
Distribution Since 1986

Cedar Fort, Incorporated

CFI Distribution • CFI Books • Inside Cougar Report

Cover Design by Corinne A. Bischoff
Lithographed in the United States of America

To Diana

TABLE OF CONTENTS

INTRODUCTION

BY LEE NELSON

I remember taking an undergraduate philosophy class at the Berkeley campus of the University of California during the early 1960s. The teacher was an atheist who delighted in challenging students' religious beliefs.

"If there's a life after death," he said at the beginning of class one day, "Why hasn't anyone ever come back to tell about it?" The students were silent for a long time. No hands went up. No one dared an attempt at answering the professor's question. With the silence, the teacher confirmed his belief that human life is snuffed out at death.

Recently, I have wished many times I could go back to that class, taking with me the knowledge of near death experiences (NDE), and all that has been published on the subject in the 1980s and 1990s.

Today, I could answer the professor's challenge.

I would tell him that many people have come back from the other side of death to tell about it. I would tell him about a recent Gallop poll which concluded as many as eight million Americans have died and come back to tell about it.

When my publisher first contacted me about writing a book on near death experiences, I told him I would if I could find enough people who had had these kinds of experiences. That same afternoon, while at one of my son's soccer games, I obtained three referrals, names of people I should call who had these kinds of experiences. In the months to come I found four stories in my own neighborhood, people whom I had known for years.

After my first book on NDEs was published, I received many invitations to speak. Over the years, whenever I am speaking to a group of more than about 200 people, I like to ask if anyone in the audience has had a near death experience. Instead of asking people to raise their hands, I ask them to come and talk to me afterwards. I can never remember a time when one or two people have not come forward.

Dr. Michael Sabom, an Atlanta cardiologist, monitored hundreds of heart patients who died, and

were later revived. Nearly half of the patients inter-
viewed claimed to have left their bodies. Some could
describe their own operating procedures in detail.
They knew where doctors and nurses were standing in
the operating room. They remembered the readings
on the life support machines. Some could even
remember the golf scores doctors were discussing
while performing surgery. Of the patients who did not
claim to leave their bodies, serious errors were made
in trying to describe the events surrounding their surgeries.

I found a typical near death experience in a
nursing journal about a man in Switzerland who found
himself in a fatal automobile accident while driving to
a championship soccer match. The first thing he
remembered after the accident was floating in the air
above the crash scene. He could see his mangled car,
which was blocking traffic in both directions. He saw
an ambulance, and a white blanket covering the
remains of his physical body which had died in the
accident.

He was obviously concerned at having died, and
wondered what would happen next. Then he could
hear voices, but not angelic ones. Angry words were
coming from the cars which couldn't move forward

because of the accident. His fellow soccer fans were upset about missing the beginning of the match, and were cursing him for making them late. Some of the drivers were actually swearing at him.

Then, through all the angry words, he heard a woman's voice offering a very sincere prayer that the man under the blanket, regardless of his religious beliefs, would be made whole, that the minds and hands of the paramedics and doctors would be guided in their efforts to heal this accident victim. It was too beautiful of a day for this man to die.

The man was so touched by the prayer on his behalf, coming from a total stranger, that he decided he would try to help the woman see her prayer answered. He willed himself down to the ground, and somehow pushed himself back into his body. He was able to get the attention of the paramedics by wiggling a toe. Fluids and drugs were administered. He lived.

Months later, after a long and painful recovery, the man asked an attorney friend to visit him. The soccer fan told all that had happened on the day of the accident, including how he was touched by the woman's prayer.

"I want you to find her for me," he told the attorney. "I want to meet her, and talk to her."

"Impossible," the attorney said. "There were hundreds of cars at the scene of the accident. Nobody took roll."

"I can make your job easy," the man responded, and handed the attorney a piece of paper with the woman's license plate number written on it.

I wonder how the Berkeley professor would explain the origin of the license plate number.

The thousands of near death experiences published in recent years provide overwhelming evidence that there is indeed a life after death. These NDEs are not considered absolute scientific proof, but constitute a growing mountain of evidence that the flame of life is not snuffed out at death—the basic premise upon which most religions are based. This is important to know, because how we view death, to a large degree, determines, not only how we live life, but how we face death.

I receive regular mail from people, who having lost a loved one, find comfort in reading the near death experiences of others. After interviewing over a hundred people about their near death experiences, and reading probably hundreds of similar experiences, I have come to the irrevocable conclusion that the world beyond this one is so different that we cannot

understand it with the same assumptions and thinking we take for granted in understanding this world.
As soon as I think I have reached a safe conclusion, I
run into someone who has had an experience that
makes me realize I still do not see the entire picture.

It seems everyone who has the opportunity to
go there, and return, sees the world beyond a little differently, depending on that person's experience and
perceptions. Only by studying a large variety of experiences enjoyed by a wide range of people can we begin
to understand and comprehend that beautiful world.
That's why books like this find a meaningful place in
the literature surrounding near death experiences.

There is nothing new about near death experiences unless it is the number of books, articles and
movies being written on the subject. People have been
having NDEs as long as written history has been kept.
King David in the Bible talks about walking through
the "valley of the shadow of death" (Psalms 23:4). He
is possibly referring to the valley or tunnel so many
people describe passing through at the moment of
death.

The apostle Paul in the New Testament was
more exact, saying, "I knew such a man, (whether in
the body, or out of the body, I cannot tell...) he was

caught up into paradise and heard unspeakable words, which it is not lawful for a man to utter" (II Corinthians 12:3-4).

In doing research for a biographical novel on Walkara, a Ute Indian chief, I uncovered what appeared to be a classic out-of-body experience. Walkara told the story to early trappers and later to the pioneers who settled in his homeland.

As a young man, Walkara went high into the Uinta Mountains in search of the Great Spirit, Towatts. The chief said his soul was troubled following the killing of some men from a neighboring tribe. He went to the mountains fasting, hoping for some kind of communication with Towatts, possibly to receive a medicine dream.

After several days of prayer and meditation, Walkara describes leaving his body and traveling to the world of spirits where he was greeted by Towatts, who instead of wearing buckskins, was dressed in flowing white robes. The Great Spirit gave Walkara a new name, and told him that someday a tribe of white people would come to settle in Ute lands, and he should not make war with them.

Walkara was happy in the world of spirits and did not want to return to mortal life, but Towatts told him he must, so he did. Later, when the settlers arrived in Ute lands, Walkara led a band of two hundred well-armed warriors, and probably could have driven the white settlers out, but didn't, because of his medicine dream, or what appears to be a near death experience.

After reviewing numerous NDEs, many of which were not published in this book for various reasons, some common elements seem to surface. If a model or typical example could be created, it would go something like this.

At the ultimate point in pain or agony, the subject suddenly finds himself/herself separated from the body, usually in the air above the body looking down. We call this experience death. If the subject is in the hospital, he/she can see the doctors or attendants frantically trying to revive the body, or he/she can hear them pronouncing the body dead—but cannot see or hear the spirit. The new spirit body is found to be different, consisting of a finer spirit matter that allows the individual to pass through walls or other physical objects.

The individual travels through a tunnel or valley, often alone, and is greeted at the other end by a spirit person or escort, sometimes clad in white robes.

Some cannot remember a tunnel. If color is mentioned, it is vivid and frequently green.

The subject then approaches some sort of barrier, like a door to a large room, where he or she might be greeted by former acquaintances who have died. These individuals do not have wings, normally do not sing in choirs, but seem busily engaged in important work.

Sometimes the subject gets a glimpse of another part of the spirit world where spirits are not happy. Sometimes scenes from the subject's life are flashed before his or her eyes, a heavenly version of instant replay. There is an intense feeling of love, joy and peace in a world where time is not measured. Most often communication takes place without words, the subject and those about exchange ideas through thought only, like they are reading each others' minds.

When the subject is informed that his/her time to die has not yet arrived, that he/she must return to the physical body, there is usually reluctance to go back. When the spirit re-enters the body, the former pain and suffering returns. As a result of the NDE, the subject usually loses fear of death.

As touched on earlier, this book does not provide absolute proof that there is life after death. But it does contain substantial evidence in the form of personal experiences of individuals who slipped beyond their physical bodies and somehow returned, bringing with them the memory of what happened on the other side. The individuals, whose stories are told in this book, come from all walks of life, all ages, different religious beliefs, both the rich and the poor, some with college degrees, others who did not finish high school.

As you read these stories, imagine yourself in the role of the interviewer, sitting across the table, or next to the subject on a living room sofa. You are listening carefully while the subject relates a sometimes sacred experience, perhaps an experience the subject has been reluctant to share with others for many years, possibly for fear of being laughed at. But the subject is telling it to you, maybe with some hesitation, at times filled with emotion, even to the point of shedding a few tears.

As you listen, you can feel the sincerity of the subject as he or she relates the near death experience. You may be a little skeptical at first, but out of politeness and consideration you allow the person to tell the complete story. Occasionally you ask a question.

After interviews with two or three people, you might still have some reservations about the truthfulness of what you are hearing, but after 18 interviews you realize that all these people couldn't be fabricating fiction. Sure, the people were under extreme stress when they had their experiences, but there are simply too many parallels, too many common elements, too many threads of truth tying the stories together. You find yourself in agreement with the subjects, firm in the belief of a very real and tangible afterlife.

Lee Nelson

CHAPTER ONE

A WORLD OF EXPLODING COLOR

In 1965, on the way home from Christmas shopping, our car ran out of gas. My husband parked the car on the side of the road and went for gas. I had the three older children in the back seat, and the youngest one, Paulette, with me in the front seat.

I don't know exactly why, but I had the intuition to hand her to her sister in the back seat. Immediately after I did this our car was hit. The man in the other car was going 75 miles per hour in a 30 mile per hour zone when he hit us. He knocked our car across the highway toward the median. The door on the driver's side flew open and I was thrown onto the pavement. The car then bounced back off the median and rolled on top of me.

I guess I was unconscious for a long time. I

don't remember much of anything after I saw the car coming at me, but when I woke up I knew I was on the ground. I couldn't figure out exactly what had happened.

"I'm just going to lay over the top of you mom," I remember my son, Jerry,saying, "in case the car blows up."

"If it hurts," he continued, "tell me."

I hadn't felt pain yet. I was dazed, wondering what would happen next. In time, an ambulance arrived and took me to the hospital. By the time I reached the emergency room, the pain was really starting to set in.

I remember feeling very detached from everything. I was broken in so many places they didn't know if I was strong enough to stand the additional stress of surgery. At this point, I thought I was dying.

"We better do something because I'm getting a straight line," I heard someone say. Then I passed out.

The next thing I remember is being up in the air, looking down at the doctors and nurses gathered around someone on the table. Suddenly, I realized it was me. It took a while for the reality of what was happening to sink in.

"What am I doing up here?" I asked myself,

while watching the doctors doing all kinds of things to me. "Well, I guess I died," I finally concluded.

And then, all of a sudden, there was a bright light, like nothing I had ever seen before. It wasn't like a flood light, or high-beam headlights shining in your eyes. Nothing like that at all. It was a beautiful, soothing light. It was warm, and I wanted to go to it.

As I started moving to the light, there were people everywhere, some of them talking. They were all along this path that I was on. They were going to the light, too. I can't remember recognizing any of them. But I remember clearly, there were people everywhere.

Everything was clear, sharp and bright. There were no dull colors. All the colors were vibrant, almost like they were exploding into my vision. Even the flowers along the path were bright and beautiful.

And there was music too—words cannot describe the beauty, simplicity and majesty of the sound. The music was neither loud nor soft, just a serene, penetrating sound that ran through every particle of my soul.

The people along the path were not wearing normal clothes. They were dressed in bright, white clothing. The women were wearing something like an A-frame dress that was loose and flowing, almost like a robe. The material was beautiful. It seemed to be glowing. The men's clothing was similar yet more manly, almost like a full-body toga. The men's clothes were made of the same iridescent cloth as the women's.

I just continued along the path, soaking in the wonderful music, looking at the beautiful colors and people. As I continued along, the light seemed to be getting stronger and warmer.

Finally I came to a beautiful person who stepped in front of me, and said, "You need to go back."

All the people I saw were bright and beautiful, but this person was somehow brighter. I think I was standing face to face with Jesus Christ, but I don't know for sure.

"You have to go back," he said. But I didn't want to go back. Everything was so beautiful here, and I knew if I went back there would be lots of pain.

"What if I don't want to go back?" I asked.

"You have children to raise," he said. "You have something you have to do. Your life is not through. You can't come here, not yet."

"Okay, if I have to go, I guess that's what I'll do," I decided. But I hesitated. I didn't want to go back. It was tough to even think about leaving that beautiful place. But then I thought about my children, especially my youngest daughter who was still so little.

So I went back. But this time it was not a journey. One minute I was in this beautiful, bright paradise, thinking about my children, then suddenly there was a big thud, a bang, like I was hitting a brick wall. I woke up and all the pain was there. It was terrible.

I spent about nine weeks in the hospital, including seven weeks in traction and three in rehabilitation to get over my addiction to all the morphine they had been giving me for pain.

I couldn't walk, and they told me I would never walk again. My left hip had been dislocated and my pelvis had been broken in both the front and back. And to top it off the bottom disc in my spinal column had been shoved up one and a quarter inches. Despite this, I was furious when they told me I would never walk again. I had two doctors taken off my case because I was determined to recover fully and I didn't need the doctors telling me I couldn't.

Four years later, with the help of a lot of therapy I was finally able to walk again. I still can't run, and I am always in pain, but I have accomplished my goal and proved the doctors wrong.

Since my recovery I have felt a real connection with the next world. I feel a closeness, a kinship to loved ones who have passed to the other side.

Lois C.

CHAPTER TWO

STAR VALLEY, WYOMING

On May 27, 1977, I was on my way to our place in Star Valley, Wyoming. With me was my daughter, Carol, and my two grandsons, Ryan and Chet. I had picked up the boys at 9:30 a.m. The last thing I remember that morning was getting in the car and closing the door.

An hour later we were involved in a serious accident. I remember being on my left side, going through some twisting movements.

When I finished twisting, I had a feeling of rising. At the same time I felt like I was free at last. I felt great. I saw green all around me. As I looked down I could see Star Valley. It was absolutely beautiful, and green beyond description. I had the ability to see all around me at once. I could see no visible signs of roads. As I moved or floated about, I could hear many beautiful sounds, such as birds singing. I moved very smoothly in an upright position. I seemed to be in a hurry, moving along in a specific direction over the valley.

The vegetation and colors were very different from what we know here. There is no way to describe or express fully what I saw and felt. But I was seeing much more than Star Valley.

As I traveled along, I came to a home. It was a two-story house with a very steep roof and was set in an east-west direction. I entered the house, but not through a door. I don't seem to remember any walls or doors. I just walked toward the house, and then I was inside.

There were two people there, and they were not surprised to see me. It was as though they had been expecting me. I recognized their faces. It was Aunt Hattie and Uncle Matthew Allaman. They were happy to see me. We hugged and kissed each other, and then I continued on my way. I was in some sort of hurry, but I can't remember why.

As I moved along, I saw a few people whom I had known when I was young, but had since died. I waved to them and went on my way. They knew me, too. They were all Star Valley people, and many had been neighbors to my grandparents. Some I knew only by face and not by name.

Soon, I came to a house I didn't recognize. It was a two-story home similar to Grandma and Grandpa Yeaman's house, but it wasn't theirs. As I came close, I saw my father walking towards one of the rooms that was very large and open. He was healthy and in excellent condition. I could see him in perfect detail. I saw him first, and then my mother. The next thing I remember, we were all hugging. My father was about the same age he was before he got the illness that eventually took his life. My parents were dressed in normal, casual clothes that they had worn every day. The room had high ceilings, but there were no sharp corners.

We continued to hug each other. I was very happy to see them and they were happy to see me, too. And they were not at all surprised. Interestingly, I could not see my mother as clearly as I could my father.

But I told them I was in a hurry to see Grandma. My parents showed nothing but love for me while I was with them. They didn't try to get me to stay. They acted as though they had been expecting me. And they looked the same as I remembered them in this life.

I hurried on towards my Grandma Beutler's home. I went through a trellis with beautiful green vegetation on it and in front of it. The arched gate at one end was open. Then I turned east. The vegetation was still lovely. I saw a couple of more people and I waved to them. I saw my Grandma's house and it was the same house I had known as a child. It was red and white, and was exactly like it had been when I was little. I didn't go into the front door, but walked between the house and garage. I saw the little house by the garage that they rented, and it also was red and white. I saw this as I walked towards the house.

I went around to the back and entered through the back door. I didn't open the door. I just walked in. I was on the back porch and looked into the kitchen. Then, I walked through the kitchen door.

I saw Grandma standing over an old fashioned wood burning stove that had a warming oven full of large plates. She was probably cooking something. She had some type of covering on her head like a scarf or a night cap. There was no brim or ties under her chin. She wore a full apron. On each shoulder there was a tan ruffle, about the same color as a gunny sack.

Grandma looked up from the stove and saw me

standing there. We went towards each other and embraced. She took me and loved and petted me, like she used to do when I was a child. She was very happy to see me. And, I felt like a little girl again when I was with Grandma. I was relieved to be there and told her I was glad that I had finally made it. I was completely at peace.

I told Grandma I was overwhelmed to be there. She told me she was glad to see me, and that I could stay and rest for awhile, but that I would have to go back. I could not stay with her.

She then took me through the dining room and into the living room towards the couch in front of the window. She had me lay down on the couch with my head in her lap. She held me and loved me. Next thing I remember, I stood and she fussed with my hair a little. Then she said it was time for me to leave. We both went out through the dining room, into the kitchen, and out the back door.

We walked to the front of the house, and continued to the place where I first remember coming into the valley. Grandma and I stood together on the crest of a hill. When I went down the hill, she stayed at the top. We never said goodbye, and I never looked back.

As I went down the hill, I felt myself going through the same twisting motions I had experienced earlier. I seemed to be struggling to get back into a certain position. This is the only memory I have about the accident.

I was told I was in a very serious condition when the policeman arrived at the scene of the accident. When the policeman saw me, his first thought was that I was dead. He began to work on me. Some said that if the policeman had not arrived as quickly as he had, I would probably have died. Even though I was thrust abruptly back into the pain, the feelings of love, peace and comfort have remained with me for quite a long time.

Hortence H.

CHAPTER THREE

HILL 681, VIETNAM

I spent my 19th birthday in boot camp, my 20th and 22nd in Vietnam. My first year in Vietnam was 1966. I got wounded, was taken out of the country, recuperated in Okinawa, and rotated back to the States when my thirteen months were up. I was here about four or five months and since I am not a state-side Marine I got bored, so I volunteered to go back. I arrived for the second time in Vietnam in February of 1968, in time for the last part of the Tet Offensive.

When the offensive was finished I was in Hue City. We were pulled back to a rest camp for a couple of weeks and were then flown by helicopter two clicks north of Khe Sanh where we were to run patrols around the exterior skirt of the area.

We were there about a month when we were sent north to Hill 881. There again, like every other place we had been we ran patrols. We went up there with a reinforced company of between twenty and forty men. During the routine patrols there were periodic rocket attacks, mortar attacks, and things like that. We began losing quite a few men.

Then during July everything started to happen. On the 3rd, the company commander got word from the battalion that we were going to evacuate the hill and return it to the North Vietnamese. This didn't make us happy, because a lot of people had died taking that hill.

We were ordered to tear down all our bunkers and all our trench lines–anything that could protect our bodies from being hurt. We had to tear down or blow up everything. The next day army helicopters were supposed to come pick us up and move us to another hill, 681, further to the east. But they never showed up, so essentially we were naked against attacks from the North Veitnamese Army (NVA). We could have called in naval gunfire, artillery, or air strikes, but the idea that we didn't have anyplace to hide kind of made people ugly.

On July 6th the army helicopters, I think it was

the 101st, came over and picked us up late in the day. They dropped us off just outside the perimeter of Hill 681, so we had to walk up the hill. That evening we got into a firefight. Normally firefights would only last a few minutes since they were used as an NVA method of finding our weak spots, but this night would be different. This time the North Vietnamese were trying to get through our barbed wire to kill us.

I carried fifteen magazines of 20 rounds each. I also had with me six hand grenades, three of which were white phosphorus grenades. These ignite and burn brightly. The only way you can put it out if it gets on you is by putting mud on it to deprive it of air. If you take the mud off, it starts burning again. It will burn straight through you as long as it has oxygen, and that's why we used them.

By the time morning came around I didn't have anything left, except for maybe one magazine. Everyone else in the trenchlines was in the same predicament. None of us had any ammunition. Everyone was tired and ornery. By then I had adopted the attitude of, "I'm going to do everything I can to stay alive. But if I die, no big deal." Everybody was complaining that they didn't want to go over to the ammo dump and bring some ammo back down to the line. So, finally I said, "Oh, what the hell, I'll do it." I got up and walked clear over to the opposite side of the hill, maybe 200 yards. I made one run carrying back small arms ammunition. The next runs were to bring back eight-one mortar ammunition. Each box of this ammo weighs about sixty pounds. It was my third trip back, and I was carrying a box in each hand. I didn't want to stay out in the open too long, because their snipers were watching us.

Then the North Vietnamese started bombing us with rockets, and one of them exploded right behind me. I never heard a thing. It picked me up and threw me down the hill twenty feet. Shrapnel caught me in both feet, both legs, both hip pockets, both hands, both arms, the small of the back and back of the head. I landed on my knees. When I landed I had my right arm tucked behind me. I was still conscious. I shook my head and looked over and couldn't see my arm. All I thought was, "Damn! Those suckers blew my arm off! They're really trying to kill me!" These were the type of things that were running through my mind.

I reached over with my left hand and pulled my arm around. Of course my arm was there, but it was really chewed up. With my left hand I grabbed my right arm and cradled it across my chest. When I did this my hand went inside the gaping wound in my right arm. My right arm was split open and bleeding like a stuck pig. I got up and started walking back up the hill. One of the men I knew who was sitting in a foxhole looked up and said, "Damn! Look at your legs!" I looked down and all I could see was blood. Down I went, flat on my back. The explosion had taken my helmet off. Where it landed I don't know. My flak jacket was still on, but my back was really torn up.

When the corpsman finally came up he took off my flak jacket and stopped the bleeding in my arm. He attempted to stop the bleeding in my legs. I was really hurting. I had my eyes closed and was gritting my teeth. The pain was starting to catch up with me. I really didn't want to look at my body because I was afraid I was missing parts. I heard somebody say, "Why don't you give him some morphine for the pain?" But, the corpsman couldn't because of the risk of shock. It would have just leaked back out anyway.

While all this was happening, I was telling myself I didn't want to die. Then I was talking to the Lord saying, "God, this hurts too damn much to stay alive." I was waffling back and forth. One of the guys said "Cheer up, you're going home." I said "I'll tell you what, if I'm going home this way, you can take my place and I'll stay here. Okay?"

I started getting really tired, physically tired, and I said to myself, "I've had enough of this. I'm tired. I want to go to bed, and I want to go to sleep." I quite literally gave up. It was no big deal. That was it. I knew they couldn't stop me from bleeding. I knew I was really torn up. It was just my time to die. So I relaxed.

The next thing I knew, there was no pain. Absolutely no pain. And I felt light and really warm. It was like when you are sitting in the shade on a nice warm day.

I saw this light coming toward me, and I thought to myself, "This is really weird." As the light approached I started seeing shapes—trees, grass and a river, all in full living colors that stunned my senses. As I got into the light even more I looked down and was shocked to see that my feet weren't on the ground! I wasn't really walking, yet I was moving right along toward this river.

When I reached the river I couldn't proceed any further. On the other side there were fields and things. I could see people on the other side, but I couldn't see them well enough to identify them. However, I could see that they were all dressed differently. Some were in everyday street clothes, some were in pure white and others looked kind of ragamuffin. Their clothes weren't really tattered, but they obviously were not the best.

I stood there and looked at them for awhile. A few turned toward me and started waving from across the river. Then they started beckoning me to come across the river. I wanted to go forward and go across the river. The water was the clearest water you've ever seen in your life. The harder I tried to move forward the more resistance I met. These people kept saying "Just come! Just come!" There was this one individual in particular that I noticed. He was one of the men who was with me there in Vietnam who had died. When he had died half of his face was blown away. I could see a great big grin on his face, the way I remembered him before he died. This guy was always into mischief. He was worse than me.

"Come on over!" he said. "You'll know everything that I know."

When he said that, things started coming into my mind. I knew why I died. I knew why there were illnesses. I knew when the cures were going to be. I knew why human beings are as stupid as they are. Any question I could think of, I knew the answer to. The feeling was really overwhelming. Answers were coming into my mind for questions I had never wondered about before. The more I thought about it the more I wanted to go on to the other side of the river. As I struggled to move forward I felt this hand come on my right shoulder. When the hand touched me I felt this endless love and endless caring. I couldn't turn to see who it was. A voice came. It was a very soothing voice, very, very soothing. The voice said, "You can't go."

I replied "Tough. I want to go. I don't want to go back. I want to go there."

The voice said, in a very quiet and subdued tone, "You can't go. You have to go back. Your time on earth isn't over yet. You have things to accomplish." As quick as he said that, boomerang, I was back!

I opened my eyes. The pain was there. I was still laying on the ground. The corpsman was pounding on my chest trying to get my heart going. He kept on saying to me, "Don't you die on me, you son of a bitch!" I found out later that I had lost nearly half of my blood. I lost so much blood that one of the corpsmen later said to me, "There wasn't enough blood in your body to keep you alive. Why you're alive is beyond us."

David H.

CHAPTER FOUR

BLACK SPOTS ON A WHITE ROBE

By the time I was fourteen I had been involved with drugs for quite a while—since I was about nine or ten. I did not actually start using drugs heavily until I was in Junior High, and by then I was doing quite a few things that I shouldn't have been doing. I was really not a very nice person.

One evening in particular I had gotten together with some friends at my house to do some drugs. They had bought a bag, an ounce, of marijuana for us to smoke. I didn't know it at the time because they didn't tell me, but the marijuana had been laced with opium, or "dipped." When things got going we decided to have a contest to see who could smoke the most. I won. They passed out, but I continued on, thinking I was doing really great. When I had finally had enough I remember crawling to my room. I crawled onto my bed, and the whole time I couldn't think straight at all.

The next thing I remember, I was seeing my body lying on the bed. I didn't realize it at first. I was thinking, "This is my room, and there is someone lying on my bed." Then I thought to myself, "I don't feel stoned anymore." Everything was very clear, very sharp, and I thought that was really unusual. I was more sober than sober, and I was acutely aware of my surroundings and feelings. After a couple of seconds of wondering who the person was on my bed I suddenly realized that it was me. At that point I realized that I had died. I thought to myself, "I'm going to have a real hard time explaining this to my mom." I was afraid that she was going to be really mad at me, maybe not so much for dying, but for the way that I had died, for overdosing on drugs. I thought, "I am in trouble." It is kind of funny that I was having these thoughts, but I was still in the frame of mind of a fourteen-year old.

Then I began being pulled through this roundish tunnel. I remember thinking it was the fastest elevator I had ever been on. I could feel it. I could hear it. It was something like wind. The space I was in was just barely bigger than myself. Up ahead in the distance I could see a light. It looked like it was around a corner or something. I started moving faster and faster when all at once I was there at the light, in a room.

It was not a big room, but it was full of people. Some were sitting on chairs and others were standing. It reminded me of bleachers. The surprising thing was that all of these people were laughing at me. I looked down to see what they were laughing at and noticed that I had this white robe on. As I looked more closely I noticed that there were these large black spots on the side of my robe. It was then that I knew what they were laughing at. These spots represented the things that I had been doing. I was really embarrassed. Their laughing hurt my feelings, so I tried to hide the spots by crouching down, but they just started laughing harder and harder. They knew what I was trying to do and how I was feeling. I was humbled and all I wanted was to disappear.

The next thing I knew, the laughing quieted down, and then stopped. I looked up and saw a very bright light coming towards me. This light was coming from a man who, when he reached me, put his comforting arms around me. Although it was not communicated to me explicitly I know without a doubt that this man was Jesus Christ. At this point I

was feeling a little more secure and a little less embarrassed. He then asked me if I knew what I was doing
was wrong. I did, so I said "Yes." At this point he was
still holding me, hugging me like a dad would hug his
daughter. This is when the review of my life started.
It was more of an emotional type of review than a
judgment. I was reliving all the remorse, all of the
pain and all of the feelings that I had felt. It was
extremely intense.

Throughout the whole ordeal there was nothing
but love radiating from the man whose arms were
around me. All the negative feelings and emotions
were coming from me. I was the one feeling the negative things, and I was the one generating them. After I
felt all those things a wave of love, supreme love, pen-
etrated my being almost to the point of being overwhelming. I knew that this man loved me even
though I had done all those bad things, some of which
were pretty rotten. Those feelings of love I will
always remember. Each one of the cells in my body
was excited. His love healed the pain, and my cells
were joyous.

At that point I had to make some decisions. I
was shown the kingdom. I didn't want to leave it, but
I knew that I wouldn't be able to progress from where

I was at the moment. I knew that I wouldn't be able to get to where I wanted to be. It came to me that the most important thing I had to do was that I had to bring people back to him. It was then that I remember him hugging me again, and just holding me. During this embrace I communicated to him that I wished to return to my life. I was immediately returned to my body, at which time I woke up to find that it was already morning.

I didn't dare tell anybody of the experience because of the nature of what I had done, overdosing on drugs. I was afraid of getting into big trouble. But one day I did mention my experience to one of the leaders of my church. He told me that I had just had a dream. He said it was like one of the dreams the prophets have in the scriptures. I knew for certain, however, that what I had experienced was anything but a dream. After that I did not tell anybody about my experience for a very long time because I was afraid of how they would react. I knew they would think that I was crazy. I felt like in their minds I was not worthy of such an experience.

I kept everything inside for a long time. In fact, I was probably about twenty before I told my mom. One reason for this was that I didn't know of anyone who had had the same type of experience. I just didn't feel like anyone would believe me. Even when I started telling people about this experience, it was all so personal that it took a long time before I could speak about it without getting really emotional. Even now when I think about it, it all comes back to me.

When I finally broke down and told my mom, she believed me. I was surprised because it wasn't until much later that I was able to tell the rest of my family what had happened to me.

At this point in my life I feel comfortable with what happened to me. At fourteen you are a little unstable, especially when it comes to something like this, but now I have had time to mature and contemplate the events of my near death experience, and I can see how I have grown from it.

Through the years, however, the memories of this experience have never faded. I have not ever rationalized those events into being a dream, nor will I ever be able to do such a thing. Everything was too real. There is no question in my mind. And besides, dreams don't change people's lives as drastically as this experience changed mine. The morning after I woke up from the experience I was different. It was immediate. Among other things, from then on I chose not to do drugs.

All this, combined with me being a typical four-teen-year old, made it a very trying time for me. One thing that I found especially difficult was that after I had felt so much love, when I came back, to mortality, I couldn't feel anybody's love for me. I assumed that if I couldn't feel the same love from others that I did from that spiritual being, then they must not really love me. Having felt such immense love there, and then coming directly back to the mortal world where love is not perfect, just made things worse.

I had always assumed that when I was a mother I would experience that same type of love for my children, but now that I am a mother I have grown to accept the fact that not even a mother's love for her children resembles the overwhelming feeling of love I experienced on the other side. The concept finally came to me that maybe we are not capable of that type of love here, and that maybe people really do love me here in mortality. Before I came to this realization I was probably a difficult person to be with. In fact, I was actually very depressed after my experience. I just wanted to get back to the love. I also felt like something was missing from my experience, almost as if there was something that I had seen or something I had agreed to which had been erased from my memory.

A few years ago, however, this blank space came back to me and has really helped me in dealing with my life. It was at a time when I was really upset about all the health problems I was having. I was pondering over these things one day when suddenly it hit me that my health problems were a decision I had made—I had decided to accept health problems as part of my earthly trial. I had learned of this trial when I was having my experience, and I still consciously made the decision to return to my body and accept what was intended to happen to me.

Another interesting effect the experience had on me was the state of alienation it put me in with my peers. When I woke up that morning my same friends were still in the house, so I was presented with the task of informing them as tactfully as possible that I no longer did the kinds of things we had been doing. I had really had a sudden change of attitude.

When I got old enough to go to high school, I didn't fit in very well. I was unpopular and didn't have any real friends. But, by then I had become stronger spiritually. I had become more comfortable with what had happened to me during my visit to the other side. The experience gave me a second chance at life and helped me get my feet going down a more productive path.

Liz C.

CHAPTER FIVE

MY SPIRIT BLED THROUGH MY SKIN

I never knew my real mom very well. When I was about three or four years old, my mother and father divorced. My mother couldn't take care of us and my father could, so she more or less consented to having my father raise me and my brother, who was a year younger than myself.

My father married a wonderful woman I call Mom. My father was Catholic, so when I was about three years old I was baptized. I went to church with my grandmother all the time and I was always plaguing her with questions.

We lived in southern California, and one year, when I was about eleven or twelve, we made one of our regular trips to Utah to visit one of my mother's sisters. While we were there the weather was really hot. So one day we kids asked for permission to go swimming. We were given permission, but we were told that no one would take us, that we had to walk. It was a couple of miles, but we were young and would have done anything to go swimming. When we got to the pool we paid our money and walked through the building to the water. As we approached the pool we noticed these signs that read "No life guard on duty. Swim at your own risk." We just kind of laughed at it. My sister, my cousins and I jumped in and started swimming around. Pretty soon we were in the deep end and decided to have a race. They said, "Oh Lucinda, you're such a good swimmer, you'll just beat us all. We don't want to race." So, I said "Okay, I'll do the butterfly and you guys just swim normally. Will you do that?" "Sure," they said. So we started off across the pool.

When I reached the middle of the pool I got cramps in both my calves and my thighs, so it was like having four cramps at once. I knew if I rubbed them hard and relaxed I could make them go away, but as soon as I finished rubbing one and started rubbing the other one, the first one would cramp up again. Very quickly I got tired of treading water and trying to rub my legs simultaneously. I was trying to reach for the side where my girl cousins were. Their arms, which were stretched out for me to grab, were only inches away, and yet it might as well have been miles. The boys were in the pool and the girls kept screaming to them, "She's drowning! She's drowning!" The guys thought we were kidding and playing around. I came up once and gasped for air, and by this time I was completely exhausted. I went down and up again and took a breath of air, but this time all I got was a mouthful of water. It went down my lungs, and I went down again. In the middle of my underwater coughing and struggling I said to myself, "I am going to die." I knew I was going to die. Within that split second, everything I had done that morning which led up to that moment slipped through my mind just as fast as a snap. It was only that morning I saw, not my entire lifetime.

I was out of air and utterly exhausted, so I began to relax. As I did I buckled into a fetus position and kind of floated in a circle. I felt like I was going into a quiet, peaceful sleep. Just at that point I remember feeling my spirit part from my body. It wasn't sucked out like I have heard other people describe. It was more like osmosis, like my spirit slowly bleeding through my skin. It was very easy.

My eyes had been closed. When I opened them

I saw that I was probably about fifteen or twenty feet above the pool. I looked down and I saw my body down in the water. As I saw my body I realized, "That's me down there. How can I be down there, while I'm up here?" I had no concept of death or what it was like, or anything. I had never heard anything about near death experiences, so I had no idea what was going on.

Everything around me was dark at that time, but off in the distance I could see something. I can't exactly call it a tunnel because I was completely surrounded by darkness, but I could see a light which my spirit was heading for. Somehow it knew that was the direction to go even though my mind didn't.

When I got on the other side it was like someone opened the door and said, "Here's the new world." I looked at it, and it was just gorgeous. It was white, so white that if I looked at the sun that would come close to matching how white it was. Then I heard something wonderful in my ears. It was singing, or music, or something. Maybe it was the angels singing, I don't know. All I do know, however, is that it was incredibly beautiful.

I could see and I could hear, so I thought I was alive. I wasn't dead, I was alive! I looked at my hands, and they were hands, so I continued traveling on. As I was traveling I came to something like a mist or a cloud, and it was also bright white. That was where I was headed, but just then something came into my head. It said, "You have to go back. You have to go back."

I answered with my mind, "I don't want to go back."

Again the male voice said, "You have to go back."

I said, "Please, I don't want to go back, I want to stay." And he said again, "No. You have to go back."

As I thought about what the voice was asking me to do I thought to myself, "If I could just get beyond that point," which was probably about ten feet in front of me, "I won't have to go back." I don't know if I actually jumped, but somehow I thrust myself toward the point of no return. I had decided that I was not going to go back to my life. I wanted to keep going where my spirit was headed. Just as soon as I thrust forward, however, my choice was taken away from me and in a split second I was back within my body, and the boys were dragging me out of the water.

I was coughing and choking while they were

asking me if I was alright. There was a group of people around me watching. And I was just rubbing my calves and thighs groaning, "Oh, my legs, my legs!"

I never said anything to anyone, not to my sister or my cousins, for years. They thought I was a strange kid anyway, so I assumed that if I told them all about what happened they would really think I was wacko. So, I kept quiet.

But one thing that I realized about my experience after I had a chance to reflect on it for a while was that while I was on the other side I was not aware of any sense of time. It seemed as if time was nonexistent. I had no idea how long I could have been there. Time, which we are familiar with, was a completely alien concept.

After my NDE, while I was growing up, I discovered that I had been given a special spiritual gift. I found that if I took a metal object that someone wore, like keys or a bracelet or ring, I could tell their past. I thought it was a pretty neat game.

When I was a senior in high school, I considered my gift pretty special. I remember the first time I ever told a girl her future. I took this object of hers, and I told her she was pregnant. She was shocked. She said "Nobody knows that but me and my girlfriend. How do you know?" And I said "I just know." I said, "And you're going to have twins." She had twins.

The more I did it, the easier it came. It got to where all I needed to do was just hold their hand, and then it progressed to the point where all I had to do was look at them. I know this sounds strange. It sounds strange to me. I told my mother about it one day and she went berserk. "Don't you ever do that again!" she said. "That's the work of the devil!" When she said that it scared me so bad that I followed her advice and never did it again. When I got a little older I tried it again, but everything was vague. Apparently I had lost the gift through unuse. Now, I haven't done it for years so I couldn't say whether I could do it at all, although I am sure if I practiced it I could get it back.

I still like to think of it as a gift I received as a result of my NDE, since I could not do those things before my experience. Also, that was not the only gift I came back with. There are a few more. I sometimes resented these special abilities I acquired because they made me different, and occasionally I would wonder if I was going insane. This is why I have tried to put a stop to all these gifts.

Anyway, the other gift was the ability to dream

and see events in the future before they happened. Sometimes I would have a dream about simple things like someone coming through a door in a certain place. So, later when I would be in that situation I could tell people who and when someone would come in through the door. Other times I could tell people what was happening on the other side of a wall because I had seen it. It was like a heightened, more regular sense of deja vu.

On one occasion I had a dream about one of my old boy friends. I dreamt that he and his family went to their ranch to ride horses. I saw that on one ride in particular his horse got spooked when he was jumping a creek. He fell off on his head, and it killed him. Then I watched the funeral.

I knew his mother well, so I went to her and I told her about my dream. I told her, "Please, please, don't let him go." She said, "Don't worry. He won't even be home when we go on our trip." He was gone and not scheduled to come home for another few months.

Well, for some reason something got goofed up and, just as I saw in my dream, he came home early and went on the trip. Everything started falling into place like my dream had shown. Finally his mother remembered what I had told her, and she said, "No, you're not going on this outing." So his father took his place and rode his horse. On the ride, the horse his father was riding went to jump a stream and got spooked. His father fell off and broke his arm. Luckily it didn't kill him. This was an occasion where my dream changed things for the better.

I had a hard time dealing with my NDE and the dreams that were associated with it, especially since I had no control over my dreams. I couldn't be myself, and I couldn't be normal. I would stay up all night and walk the house like a ghost. When I got married it really put a strain on our marriage. It was really hard for my husband to deal with how I acted. Finally it ended in divorce. I have since remarried.

On the positive side of things, since my NDE I have had numerous experiences with my relatives on the other side in helping them resolve situations here in mortality. This has been both rewarding and fulfilling for me in the sense that it has brought me closer to my loved ones who have passed on.

I have learned some very important lessons from my encounters with the other side. For a time after my NDE I was sustained by the love and joy that I had felt, but then gradually I became part of the

world again. I started once again to be judgmental, to
lose my temper and to be more negative. Then, after
going to some NDE group support meetings I was
reminded of the love we should all share, and that we
cannot allow ourselves to judge others. We are here
for our free agency. We can choose whatever we want
to do or be. It is the Lord who will judge us all. I now
feel like I must help everyone I can, even if it is nothing more than telling them that I care about them.

Lucinda H.

CHAPTER SIX

NO TUNNEL, NO LIGHT, NO NOTHING

P eople who have these near death experiences are not special or privileged, but I
think that's an idea that many people have. In fact
sometimes it tends to be more of a burden than a priv-
ilege because of the increased awareness the person
gains. The more aware you are, the more you are
tempted. So you have to be on your guard a lot more.

Having an NDE is like when you are peeking
through a crack in a door into a lighted room when
suddenly the door is thrust open and you see everything. It makes it very simple, but at the same time it
makes it very frustrating. I find myself not having
patience for games because life is too precious and too
short for games. I believe in being up front and honest
with people, and it hurts when they are not the same
way with me. But I can't judge them because spiritu-

ally that is where they are right now.

We are in a world where we must learn things one at a time, precept after precept. People who experience an NDE sometimes see geodesic shapes, and sometimes they see Christ. It all depends on what level they are on spiritually, and whether they are ready for the experience or not. God is not going to take away our freedom to choose by throwing us into something that we're not spiritually ready for and make us deal with it. Thereby we have all our different religions, we have all our different spiritual attitudes and so forth. It's all channeled for the needs of the individual, and yet it's all very similar.

My experience happened during a time in my life when I was not active in any particular religion. I had gotten pregnant out of wedlock. At that time such a thing was a real scandal. It was really a traumatic situation. I came from an abusive, single-parent home without a father. I did not have a sense of self-esteem, so I was searching for love in the arms of anyone. I got involved with this guy, and I felt that he loved me. It was the usual story.

My experience happened during childbirth. While I was in labor I got to the point where I couldn't dilate any further. I have a rheumatic heart, so I had a heart murmur that they were concerned about. Realizing the stress on me, that I wasn't going to be able to do much more, they took me in for an X-ray to see what was wrong. This revealed to them that they would have to go in and do a mid-forceps delivery. So they took me into surgery and put me out. That is when I had the experience.

I was lying on the operating table, when suddenly I wasn't. I didn't really see anything in the operating room. I was just in a maze of black. When I say black, it was as if I was in a cave. I was in pitch black with no tunnel, no light, no nothing. Then I could see these people around me. I could barely see them, though, because it was like when you are on a tour of a cave and they have lights behind the rocks and formations. It was not like there was light shining on them. Rather, it looked like it was actually radiating out from them.

To the left of me were many people whose faces I could not really distinguish, but who were all clad in white. They were all women and men who I perceived to be relatives who had died before. One of them happened to be an aunt of mine who had died three or four years earlier. I sensed her more than saw her, however.

Then on the right side of this expansive darkness were all these other individuals who I perceived
to be men and not women. They were also clad in
white, but again I couldn't distinguish their faces.

Down at the very end of wherever it was I was
standing, in the direction that I was facing, was a very
large throne-type chair. It had a high back to it, and
the arms came out in kind of a throne style. There
was a personage sitting in the chair also in white. I
knew it was a man, and yet I couldn't distinguish who
it was, except that this person was in great authority
over my life. On the left side of me was my grandfather whom I had never known in this life. My grandmother was to my right. I was just standing there.
What was being said during thought transference was,
"You have not morally lived up to the expectations
and the mission you agreed to when you came to
earth." My fate was then in the hands of the individual in the chair. His options were these: he could let
me return to life to complete my mission, or he could
let me die and not allow me to do what I had said I
would.

During this time my grandfather looked at me
and was very disappointed because of what I had done.
I have to mention at this time, my grandfather had

been extremely involved in his church for 23 years. In fact, he died while serving his church. He was a very righteous man and was not really about to plead for me. It was ultimately up to the individual in the chair to decide. My grandmother, who had died only three months before my delivery, said that she knew I could do it, that she had faith in me, and that they should give me another chance.

I threw my argument in as well to support what she had said. I said, as I was still caught up in mortal thoughts, "I know I can do it. I'm going to be an X-ray technician, and I'm going to straighten out my life. I'll do right by this baby, and I know I can do it." What I didn't know at that time was what exactly they were referring to as far as what my mission was on earth. I was totally in the dark. I just knew I wanted to live. I didn't want to die. I was very scared and panicky. Virtually all the rest of my existence hung in the balance of the decision that was to be made by the man in the chair.

Finally, the decision was made to allow me to return, but I was told that if I did not live as I was supposed to, if I did not accomplish my mission, both my child and I would die. At that time I thought they meant the child that I was having. Later it became

apparent to me that that was not the case. But as I
turned to go back into my body I saw the spirit of a
very wise, old man. To liken it to our chronological
years, he was probably in the hundreds of years old.
He had very piercing eyes and no hair that I could distinguish, and I could even see the veins in his head.
I'm making him sound grotesque, but he really wasn't.
It was obvious that he was very knowledgeable and
very wise.

As I turned to come back I saw a shaft of light
waiting to take me back. I traveled down that shaft of
light and entered my body. At that time I heard the
nurse say to the doctor, "She's back." I heard the doctor say, "I didn't think she was going to make it." So
it was nip and tuck, and even my mother told me later
on that she thought I was going to die. But, I had
made it and had a new baby daughter to show for it.

When I got home from the hospital I was very
much afraid of darkness. Here I was 21 years old and
suddenly I wouldn't sleep without a light on. I was
terrified of the dark and I didn't know why. Then little by little it came back to me what had happened. I
told my mother about it. She's the only one I really
told all about it. I had had a lot of medication during
the delivery, and I think that impaired my memory for

quite some time. It was almost a week before I started remembering the events of my experience. These memories confused me, so I didn't talk about it to anyone except for maybe two people. And it wasn't until I learned about NDEs that I realized I wasn't a nutcase.

About twelve years ago I had a little boy, and six weeks after I had him I had a dream about him. It became apparent to me that he was my mission, not my daughter as I had originally assumed. He and the mission he is to perform were the reasons I was on trial. This personal revelation came in the form of a dream, but I don't refer to these experiences as merely dreams since they are much more vivid, and contain details which I cannot forget.

In the dream he was about six weeks old, and suddenly I was standing in the doorway of an old tabernacle dwelling—the kind they had during the time of Abraham in the Old Testament. It had cloth walls supported by posts in the corners. I entered it with my husband. We were wearing modern clothes. I was holding my boy. We walked into a room where the walls were covered with a nearly white muslin-type draping. In the corners, draped from the poles, was striped, Hebrew-style material. On the floor was a Persian rug with mostly rust and red colors.

Waiting for us inside was a man. He beckoned us to come in. He was dressed in a long robe with a long Moses-like striped shawl or vest over his robe. He was also wearing a long headpiece that covered his head and had long scarf-like pieces of cloth hanging from either side. He had a long white beard and mustache. He didn't say who he was or anything. He just took my son from me, and we followed him into an adjacent room.

The light in the first room was like normal daylight, but the second room was filled with a golden light which is impossible for me to describe. The room was absolutely filled with this light. It wasn't a bright light like when you look at the sun, but rather it was like somebody had taken gold and illuminated it, or filled it with light.

The man took my infant son and laid him on an altar which was also covered with this muslin sort of swath. He laid my son down so that he was facing him, and he started to take him out of his blanket and out of his clothing. I asked him, "What are you doing?" He didn't answer. Instead he took my son's legs like a doctor would take hold of a baby's foot and pushed his leg up around to check the joints and the structure of the legs. Next he checked his arms, and then his whole body. I kept thinking to myself, "What are you doing?" I was kind of offended. Finally I asked him again, "What are you doing to my son?"

He said "I am checking him."

I asked him why, and he said, "For his mission on earth."

I then asked, "What mission is this? What are you talking about?"

He said, "All I can tell you is that he will take the place of a very wise, old man." And that is all he would tell me.

Even though Steven was only six weeks old and incapable of walking, he got down from the altar and walked over to this large font-type thing. It was like an antique bird bath hewn out of something like granite with a thick, wide lip all around it. It was very plain as well. Inside it was an oily substance, almost like oily water. My son walked over to this bath, climbed in and started swimming in it. The old man turned to me and said, "Look how unafraid he is." I said, "I know. He is swimming." He said, "Yes, he is. He is unafraid. For his mission he needs to have no fear." After he said that I woke up.

I know now that the aged wiseman I met at the

end of my NDE is my son, and that my mission is to help prepare him for his mission.

Kathleen M.

Chapter Seven

THE MOST BEAUTIFUL GARDEN

One morning in July, 1984, my husband, Vern, and I finished packing, said good-bye to our six children and two grandchildren, loaded our suitcases in the car, and were off to the Denver airport. What excitement! We were going to Europe, a vacation we had been planning for a long time.

Our first destination was Frankfurt, where our good friends Dick and Nancy Wright were going to meet us. Dick had taken time off from work so he and Nancy could show us Europe.

After a twelve-hour flight and a day's time change, we landed in Frankfurt. It was a tearful reunion. We hadn't seen Dick and Nancy for almost three years.

They lived in Dizenbach, a suburb of Frankfurt. The road went through a forest of tall, green trees.

Everywhere I looked there was lush greenery. We stopped at a little flower stand where Dick bought some flowers.

That night I had a hard time sleeping. I suppose it was excitement about being in Germany, but also there was the return of a premonition of danger that I had felt back in Colorado. I tried to push the feeling out of my mind, finally falling to sleep about 3 a.m.

The next day we began our tour of Germany. Many of the towns had cobblestone streets and quaint little shops. The roofs of the homes were covered with red tile, and the children played in Lederhosen. Our travels included Dizenbach, a cruise down the Rhine River where we saw 28 cashes in 29 miles, Koblenz, Ruttersheim, Munich, Dinkelsbuhl, Heidelberg, Rothenburg, Chemsee, and finally Bertchesgarten.

As we traveled, we stayed with the people of the country so we could get more of a feel for the places we were visiting. If someone had a room for rent they would have a sign that read, "Zimmerfrei," which translated means, "Room for rent."

Just as we entered Bertchesgarten, Dick spotted a road that led up into the mountains and turned onto it. We climbed a very steep hill, wondering if the car would be able to make the climb. Upon reaching the top, we entered the most beautiful valley I had ever seen. In the middle was a house with a sign that read "Zimmerfrei." We could hardly believe our good luck. Dick and Vern arranged for us to stay two nights.

The valley was rich and green. There was a small stream flowing through the open meadows just below the house. In front of the house was a hand-carved water trough and a pump with faces on them. Across the street from the house was a green pasture with sheep and cattle grazing. Behind the house, the mountain went straight up. At the top and to the right a little was Hitler's Eagle Nest retreat. The house we were staying in had been in our host's family for 600 years.

That afternoon we took a boat across a lake to King Ludwig's castle, followed by dinner at a restaurant in Bertchesgarten. We left the restaurant about nine o'clock in the evening. It was beginning to rain. I remember feeling those premonitions of danger again but brushed them aside.

I took hold of Vern's hand, and we started across the street. The traffic light had been turned off, so we looked both ways before crossing. We had decided to call the children in Colorado, and the only phone was at the Bonn Hoff, the old train station that once belonged to Hitler.

As we reached the far side of the street, one of my shoes fell off. We were just stepping onto the curb when I let go of Vern's hand and stepped back into the street to get my shoe. That's the last thing I remember. I was hit by a car. I was killed instantly. It was 9:10 p.m., July 28, 1984.

I don't remember being hit, but I do remember standing above my body and watching what was going on. Vern had not seen the car hit me. He only heard the thud of my body hitting the car, and the headlight glass breaking.

He turned, screaming my name, looking for me under the car. But I wasn't there. The car had hit me in the left leg just below the hip, flipping me onto the hood, pitching me forward a few feet as it came to a stop. I landed on my head, according to the report of a witness. Vern found me lying on the wet street. He called to Dick and Nancy.

They ran to me. There was blood all over. Vern gathered me up in his arms. He was screaming, "They've killed my baby, they've killed my baby."

Dick tried to console him, but Vern was hysterical by this time. Nancy ran across the street to call an ambulance.

People came from all over to see what they could do to help, but there was a language problem. They gathered up my things that had been thrown all over the street, then waited around in the event there was something else they ought to do.

Dick put my head in his hands and—even though there were no vital signs, and he knew I was dead—said a prayer. He later told me he felt prompted to do so.

I remember trying to reach out to Vern to comfort him, but I couldn't do it. I left the scene of the accident at this point and traveled through a gray mist that became lighter as I traveled upward. Eventually the fog gave way to brilliant light as I entered a beautiful garden. I don't have words to describe the beauty of the garden, but it was more beautiful than anything I had ever seen on earth, including the Koukenhoff Garden in Holland at tulip time.

I was looking for my grandmother, because I knew she would be there to greet me, but I was alone in the garden.

"My daughter, what are you doing here?" asked a voice from behind. I turned and saw a man in white whose radiance and love astonished me. He was standing in a group of trees. He began moving towards me.

As he spoke, and as I felt the love and light that radiated from him, I believed he was my Father in Heaven.
He told me that I must return to earth and put my family together again. He said that I would know my mission in life as time went on. He told me other things which I cannot repeat. I re-entered my body, in the ambulance on the way to the hospital.

A young policeman took Vern to the hospital, and Dick and Nancy came in their car. When Vern arrived, the doctors came out and asked Vern if he wanted to see the X-rays of his wife before they took her into surgery. Vern didn't know what they were talking about. He thought I was dead. He didn't know my spirit had re-entered my body in the ambulance.

The doctors then took Vern to me. I was talking to the doctors, but I don't remember this or anything else that happened for the next six weeks, except for the nightmares.

I had a ruptured spleen which was removed two days after the accident. My back was broken in two places. My pelvis was crushed and broken in four places. They said my insides looked like scrambled eggs. I was paralyzed from the waist down. Later, I lost muscle control of my arms. There was a five inch cut on my head and a large hematoma by my right eye, causing pressure on the brain resulting in a cerebral contusion. Two days after the accident my lungs collapsed. I took over 30 pints of blood, had five major surgeries in seven weeks, was on life support for three and a half weeks after that, and was kept unconscious for six weeks. I almost lost my right kidney.

Four doctors and six nurses never left me from the time I was brought into the hospital in Bertchesgarten until I left two days later for a larger hospital in Salzburg, Austria, where I spent the next two months.

At the hospital in Bertchesgarten, the doctors did two surgeries to see what organ was bleeding so badly, but since everything inside me was in such a mess, they couldn't tell where the bleeding was coming from. Since it was my spleen that was ruptured, all the blood they pumped into me just bled inside my body, swelling me up like a blimp.

When my lungs collapsed two days after the accident, Vern was at the police station filling out reports. The doctors immediately put me on a life support system, loaded me in an ambulance, and with one doctor riding with me, sent me to a large trauma and intensive care unit in Salzburg. When Vern returned to the hospital, the doctor came out and said, "She's gone." With his limited understanding of German, Vern at first thought I had died. Dick and Nancy picked up Vern and our things and headed for Salzburg.

When they arrived at the hospital, I had been in surgery again and the spleen had been removed. I was finally stabilizing. When they let Vern into the room where I was recovering from the surgery, along with several other patients, Vern had to ask which one was me. I was so blue and swollen from all the internal bleeding that he didn't recognize me. When he saw me it made him sick, and he had to leave. He told Dick and Nancy he couldn't stand to see me like that.

The doctors never gave him much hope that I would live. I was too broken up, and if I did live, they thought I would be paralyzed and have brain damage.

A week after the accident, Dick and Nancy went home, and our 15-year old daughter Marnie came to Austria so Vern would not be alone. She stayed a month.

When Vern and Marnie came each day to the hospital, they would encourage me to fight for my life, to say my prayers, and to come back to them. Marnie would rub my legs and arms so that hopefully some life would come back into them. I don't remember any of this, still being unconscious. I only remember the last several days of Marnie's visit before she had to return to Colorado.

I remember waking up at nights and not remembering where I was. I could see shadows of people and flashing lights and hear weird sounds and a foreign language. I had a nightmare that I had been kidnapped.

I would have this dream of being on a ship of some kind, of it wrecking and then being in some kind of a shed all alone. I couldn't use my legs, and I was very afraid. Then I would hear someone coming, and I would call out in my dream for Heavenly Father to give me strength to face whatever was ahead of me. I then would wake up not knowing where I was, but feeling Father's presence. I would shiver, and one of my monitors would go off, and someone would come and take my hand. Then I would feel His presence leave, and the nurse would give me something to sleep again. This happened several times, the same dream and the same happenings. Even after I came to my senses, six weeks later, the nightmares continued until I came home.

I got very close to my intensive care nurse, Ursula. On her days off I didn't do as well as when she was there. She was always encouraging me. Whenever I would wake up from a nap and not fully remember where I was, she would be there holding my hand and saying everything was okay. Before I came home she gave me a stick pin of a guardian angel, and we still write back and forth.

Another woman I got very close to was the cleaning lady in the intensive care unit. One day as I awakened, she was cleaning off my bed. She smiled at me and I back to her. Each time I would see her I would smile and she back. Then one day she took my hand and kissed it and touched my cheek. She was from Yugoslavia, speaking no English and very little German. Of course, I didn't speak her language.

We communicated through touch, smiles, and lots of love. When she would finish her day's work, she would scrub up and come back to my bed and rub my arms and legs for me. We became the very best of friends, without words. I taught her the international sign for "I love you." Each night as she left to go home she would come to the door, and we would sign it to each other.

One of my friends sent me a stuffed mouse for my birthday, but since I was in a semiconscious state at the time, Vern kept it to show me when I was fully conscious. After coming to my senses, I wouldn't believe the doctors or nurses or Vern or Marnie that I was in a hospital and very badly hurt. It was then that Vern brought me the mouse and showed it to me. I was able to get my arms up and grab hold of it, and I held it very tight to my chest. This was the first time anyone had seen me cry. Things were finally starting to make sense to me.

Ursula took the mouse from me, tied a string to the bow on its head and tied it on the bar above my bed. It was the only thing permitted in the intensive care unit that wasn't scrubbed and polished. It went everywhere with me except surgery. My cleaning lady took hold of it one day, and I told her I collected mice, and she seemed to understand. She would talk in her language, and I in mine, and we got along just fine. We became the best of friends.

Each morning several doctors came in to see how I was doing and how I felt. They would gather around my bed and would ask if I had any pain. I don't remember any pain until the day after they did the surgery to save my kidney.

One morning when the doctors came in, they all had very serious looks on their faces. I asked what was wrong. I remember that I was smiling at them as I did every time they came in. One of the doctors took hold of my hand and told me that I would never be able to walk, that my left foot had come back to normal position, but that my right foot hadn't, and that because of the nerve damage it was most likely that it never would.

I smiled at him and put my other hand over his and said it was all right. As I looked up into his eyes, a tear had formed and was on his cheek. He squeezed my hand and said, "I don't understand. I just told you that you were never going to walk again, and you're telling me it's all right? Your husband has told us how active you were, and you're smiling at us and saying it's okay?"

I looked up at him and at the other doctors and said, "I'm alive, and that's all that matters."

I told the doctors that I had told my family many times that if I had to lose a part of my body and if I had a choice, it would be my legs because if I had my hands I would still be able to do the things that I loved to do, such as hand sewing and ceramics.

"I just don't understand you," one of the doctors said. "You're smiling and telling us it's okay that you'll never walk again. Don't you ever stop smiling?"

I don't think I realized how badly I had been

hurt until the morning some nurses came in and said they needed to sit me up as I was not getting the circulation in my legs that I needed. I didn't think it would be any big deal, but I was very wrong. I couldn't sit up, at least not by myself. It took all four of the nurses to hold me up. I was like a wet noodle. It was at that moment that I finally believed what the doctors and nurses had tried to tell me, that I had been very seriously injured.

Dick, Nancy, and Vern had decided to tell me I had had a bad fall, not to let me know I had been killed and then had come back to life, but they quickly gave up on that when I began telling them exactly what each one of them had said and done immediately following the accident. It was the first time any of them realized I had had an out-of-body experience.

I never felt angry or bitter that the accident had happened. I was alive, and I was determined to be the best person I could no matter the circumstances. I was sent back to earth for a reason, and I was determined to do my best at whatever it was He wanted me to do.

After several months in the hospital, I was getting very homesick for my children. I wanted to home. The doctors kept saying that I couldn't go until I was strong enough to sit up for long periods of time. It was a 13-hour flight home. They said that sitting up that long in my present condition would kill me.

One night as I lay awake, I decided that come September 25th I was going home, no matter what, even if I had to crawl. I told Vern the next morning. He wanted to go home, too, so he said he would see what he could do. With Dick's help he found out Delta had a sleeper jet where I could lay down in flight. He reported his find to the doctors, who agreed to let me go provided I would work very hard to strengthen myself for the trip.

I had to work with rings hanging over my bed three times a day to strengthen my arms. I was taken out of bed to practice walking at least twice a day. Physical therapy sessions were increased to four times a day. These sessions included painful electric shock treatments to stimulate feeling in my legs.

The doctors, nurses, and others from the intensive care unit called nearly every day to see how I was and what I had accomplished that day. Everyone in the ward encouraged me to do better. There were lots of tears, hugs, and promises.

One night as we were in the hallway waiting for a call from the children, I was lying in the wheelchair, and Vern was talking to the nurses. A little lady in her eighties came down the hall with her crutches. We smiled at one another as we did every day in the hallway as we both were learning to use our crutches. I put my hand on hers and smiled. I had the nurse tell her that I was going home in a few days. The woman got tears in her eyes, and I put my arms around her neck and kissed her cheek. She said she must go to her room, and so I said good-bye to her and wished her well.

In a while the little lady returned to my wheelchair. She handed me a two-inch square picture of the Virgin Mary. I looked at it and started to hand it back to her, but she shook her head and pushed my hand away.

The picture was well-worn and wrinkled, and I knew it had a special meaning to her. In German, she said that over ten years ago she had gone on a pilgrimage to where the Virgin Mary was supposed to have appeared to someone in a vision or something like that and that while there everyone received a picture. She had carried it in her wallet all this time, but she wanted to give it to me now.

I thought I couldn't possibly take this possession that meant so much to her. With tears in my eyes and a lump in my throat, I told the nurse to tell her that I was very touched by her gift, but that I didn't want to take it since it meant so much to her. The little lady pushed the picture back in my hands and turned it over. In German she had written, "God bless you and your family."

Gratefully I accepted her picture. I carry it in my wallet, as she did. Every time I see it, I remember a special night of love and friendship between two people who could not even understand one another, but through love we became friends. I never saw her again, but I know we will meet in the eternities, and we will be the best of friends.

A few days before we left for home, Vern took me in my wheelchair and we visited all the people in the intensive care unit to say good-bye. We took pictures and hugged and kissed them—doctors, nurses, staff, and my little cleaning lady. It was a tearful good-bye, but I promised that I would be back, and when I came, I would walk through the doors to see them.

I had mixed emotions about going home. I wanted to go back to my family, but I would be leaving a big part of my heart in Austria. Sleep was a long time in coming that night.

I wanted to go home, and yet I didn't. I never thought it would be so hard to leave a hospital, but the doctors and nurses who had taken care of me had become very good friends. It was hard to say good-bye to them. I thanked each one for the good care they had given me and for all the help they had been to us while we were in Austria. All of them went far beyond their required duty.

We flew first to Frankfurt, where we spent the night with Dick and Nancy, then we boarded the flight for home. We changed flights in Dallas, then headed for Denver.

I had to wait until all the other passengers had gotten off and then a young man came to assist me in the wheelchair. He pushed me down the long aisle toward the room where the kids would be waiting.

All at once at the door appeared our little grand-daughter, Jacki Sue. "Grandma," she screamed as she came running to us. She threw her arms around my neck and hung onto me. I held her little hand as we went up the aisle to the doorway where the rest of the family was waiting. Everyone was there, except our son Marc who had a football game in Pueblo that night. He sent a note, hoping we would understand his absence. It was so good to see all of them again and to feel their arms around my neck. I had been so homesick for them.

The next few months were busy and happy. Friends and loved ones came by to visit or help around the house.

Each time I was able to do something for myself, tears of gratitude fell. It was so exciting to be able to once again do those things that I thought I would never do again, like feed myself without spilling food in my lap, brushing my own teeth, being able to comb my hair and then one day even dressing myself.

Two days before Halloween, I walked by myself to the living room. There was no stopping me now. Vern had sold my car thinking I would never drive again, but by January he had to get me another one.

I still have only partial feeling in my right leg, and it still has nerve damage. I have no feeling in my left leg where I was hit, but I walk. I can even run, not fast, but run. And I have gone back to racquetball. I can't play as fast as I once did, but at least I'm back on the court. My right eye becomes very blurry at times, and I have my aches and pains, but that's not serious. I'm alive.

Goals have become a very important part of my life. I believe that all righteous goals are attainable with God's help. I no longer believe in depression. I have found a joy and happiness in myself and a peace within myself that I have never had before.

My test wasn't the injuries I received in the accident or the hardships I have had to overcome. My test was how I accepted what had happened to me. I believe I had already accepted it before I came to earth.

One night as I was saying my prayers and thanking my Father in Heaven for all the blessings He had given me and for the miracles that had come into my life, a small voice came to me and said, "It really doesn't matter what your trials or tests may be here on earth. It's how you accept them. That's the real test."

I was asked once if I would change anything that has happened these past few years. My answer was no. I thought once that if I could change the pain and agony that loved ones and friends went through while I was in Europe I would change that. But the more I thought about it, I realized that perhaps that time was a test for them, too. I would not change anything. It has been the greatest thing that has ever happened to me. I am not the same person that I was two years ago.

Some mornings it would be a lot easier to stay in bed, because those first steps hurt. Some nights I don't get much sleep because my legs lock in spasms, and it is very painful. But if I give in and stay in bed, it would be easier to stay in bed the second day and much more easy the third and so on. When I get tired, I lose the vision in my right eye and the right leg drags a bit, but that just comes with the territory now. You learn to compensate and work around those things. Perhaps, in time, it will get better. Perhaps it will get worse. Whatever, I'm just grateful to be alive and doing as well as I am.

I have seen many of the things come true that Father sent me back to do. Yes, there are a few that haven't come about, and I'm still working on them. With time, patience, love, and faith, they will. After returning from the other side, I've learned that impossible things just take a little longer.

Neddie P.

CHAPTER EIGHT

MINI-INDY RACE

Hobbies have always been big in our family, especially participating in my husband's hobbies. We enjoy doing things together and I enjoy the challenge of keeping up with him. Bill has had a love for cars since childhood. His parents and friends even raced on the old Blackfoot track in Idaho in the 1960's. Before he even had a driver's license, he was the proud owner of a '57 Chevy. He still cherishes it today.

Bill had been active in building his own radio-controlled boats, cars, and airplanes, a 'B' Class Mini Tractor for a tractor pull competition, and a Mini-Indy race car. Our first activity with the race car was a get-acquainted picnic in April, 1987. The whole family felt an eager sense of anticipation. Bill's first race was in Twin Falls in May, then in Pocatello every Saturday night. In June, I joined the Ladies' Street Stock. Boyd Jenkins let me use his car for these races. It was a Camaro named "The Hustler." It was exciting, but I was never able to finish a race. There had been talk about starting a ladies' Mini-Indy race in June, but nothing had developed until the night of July 18th.

Bill, the kids and I had spent the day at a big family picnic hosted by EG&G (his employer) at the State Fairgrounds in Blackfoot. We were later than usual getting to the speedway that evening, so Bill let us out at the gate. We were seated in the grandstands when a friend, Don Beamis, came and told me of the plans for a ladies' Mini-Indy race that evening. My kids gave me encouraging hugs and "Win, Mom" wishes which I finally gave in to, but that is the last thing I remember. The rest of what I know involving my accident is what others have told me, since I personally have no recollection of the events that followed.

I had a lousy start, and I was trying hard to catch up to first place. I was going too fast for my level of experience—50 to 60 m.p.h., and going into turn number two I was too wide. I had just lapped the girl who was in last place when I realized I couldn't get the car to turn in. I side-swiped the back wall

which was made of cement road dividers. Apparently
my head hit the wall. I was unconscious when the flag
man ran to the car and shut it off. He waved for help.
Bill was one of the first to my side. When they realized I had serious injuries, they called the Life Flight
helicopter. Track officials cut off the roll bars, extract-
ed me from the wreckage and helped the paramedics
put me on oxygen in the track ambulance.

While waiting for the Life Flight helicopter, Bill
fell to his knees in prayer. Friends at the track really
pulled together at this time. Someone got our car,
others helped Bill into it and some friends got our kids
ready and waiting at the gate for the ride to the hospital. At the hospital, the doctor removed my helmet
very, very carefully and started his examination, while
Bill and the kids waited anxiously for a diagnosis. Bill
called my brothers and his family. My mother was
with a church group, so my sister-in-law, Lisa, waited
at mom's house for her return. Mom told me that she
had had an uneasy feeling that something was wrong
earlier that evening and that she felt she needed to be
home. When she saw her porch light on and Lisa
waiting, she realized her foreboding was warranted.

When they arrived at the hospital around mid-
night, there had been no change in my condition. The

doctor talked with Bill and Mom. He told them it didn't look good and that the next 24 hours would be critical. There was severe swelling on the left side of my brain, a large cut above my right eye, and two broken ribs. He told them I probably would never be like I was before the accident. Mom came in to see me for the first time. She said I was lying there motionless and cold. They all felt so helpless. Everyone knew it was in God's hands now, so all they could do was continue to pray over me.

Shortly after one of their prayers for my health, I started to vomit and show the very first signs of life. They tell me I recognized everyone and tried to talk, but the swelling on the left side of my brain left my right side numb. It was as though I had been cut in two. Even half my tongue was numb, so my words were slurred.

I slept most of the time, except for a few minutes every hour, when the nurse would wake me to ask who I was, where I was and what time it was, to keep my brain functioning. Amazingly enough, for a time after the accident, even without my glasses I could read the clock on the wall perfectly.

A few days later, Craig recited another prayer at my bedside. He told me, "I don't know where the words came from, they just came naturally. I have never felt the spirit world so close. When I was done, you opened your eyes and looked at me and said, 'Dad said I will live, I have another chance.'" Then I closed my eyes and went into a sound sleep again. Given the fact that my father had passed away in 1971, my remarks just increased my family's anxiety.

In the days that followed, I improved rapidly. By the first of August, I was ready to be moved into the rehabilitation ward. All events before that seem like fuzzy episodes from a long-ago dream. The only thing of which I have a clear memory occurred sometime during that period. I was drawn into a brilliant, bright light, and felt so peaceful. I remember sitting in a big room on a round couch, next to a man. I don't have any memory of looking at his face, but we were both in white, and watching some people, who were also dressed in white, come in and go out of the same room we were sitting in.

I remember thinking, "What are these people doing?"

He answered me telepathically, "They have their work to do."

I then thought, "What about my children?"

He told me, "They'll be taken care of."

It was the most wonderful, peaceful, loving feeling. It's almost indescribable, and I remember not wanting to leave. I was crying, sobbing, and he held me and told me not to cry—that things would be alright.

I do not know how long I was in this heavenly place, but I know I was there. Maybe I'm not allowed to remember more, like maybe looking into my dad's eyes or knowing why I was sent back to earth, but I know there was a reason for it.

The content feeling I took with me from this experience stayed with me for months. I don't remember the pain of my broken ribs or having stitches above my right eye. I vaguely remember going to Blackfoot on August 1st. I do remember coming down the hospital stairs for the first time with the physical therapist. It was so traumatic, one slow, cautious step at a time. The twenty-five mile drive from the hospital to Blackfoot that day was like an unreal deja vu, not remembering what lay ahead, but remembering the old familiar sights and places after seeing them again. The hospital sent a wheelchair with us that day, but we left it in the car. I walked unsteadily with the support of my husband's arm. Bill and the kids were so very patient, loving and helpful.

By the next week I was able to come home for the entire weekend, from Saturday morning to Sunday at 6:00 p.m. I continued to progress, and on August 21st I was released from the hospital, although I still had to go back five days a week. By November 1st I was finished with therapy, but not with the process of learning everything over again. I had lost many of my memories.

I can see and feel the progress I have made in the past two years. The main thing I have re-learned is that we shouldn't take so many things, especially the kindness of people, for granted. We need to look ahead, even though we can only take life one day at a time.

Caryn R. H.

CHAPTER NINE

HALF-IN, HALF-OUT

Because of a massive pelvic inflammatory infection my doctor told me I would never be able to have kids. My husband and I had been married six years and had no children. We were getting ridiculed so badly by everybody, including our family, that we decided we had to move. So we left for Minnesota. I was extremely ill on the ride out. It was terrible. I was throwing up violently all the time. It was then I discovered I was pregnant.

A few months later I had Jason. He was a nine pound butt breach baby, so I had him Cesarean section. It was a difficult delivery and a very difficult pregnancy. I'm a nurse, so of course everything went wrong. For example, the epidural went up instead of down. I couldn't breathe. I couldn't do anything. From the waist up I was like a quadriplegic and couldn't feel a thing, but at the same time I could feel everything down below.

I had a very difficult time after Jason's birth with postpartum blues. After about four months I was finally able to work through it, just in time to find out that I was pregnant again. It was unreal. I hadn't recovered from the first one. I didn't want any more kids after the first one. I thought, "If this is what I have to go through, forget it, I'm not doing it!" But, here I was pregnant again, throwing up and being miserable.

When my water finally broke I instantly went into hard labor with my contractions three minutes apart. There was no build up to it. It was hard labor. We got to the hospital. It was about six hours before I had the epidural, but it didn't work. So I had them redo it, but it still didn't work. I told them to redo it again a third time, and again it failed to work. Right then I realized I was in for a long haul.

The baby was turned posterior with its head turned the wrong way so it wouldn't deliver. They assured me, however, that as the labor progressed he would turn. I was hooked up to all the monitors because my first delivery had been Cesarean and had been only 14 months earlier. Ten hours into the delivery I completely dilated and had to begin pushing because the baby was starting to become a little acidotic. We needed to get the baby out.

Of course I had almost lost it by then. I would have the contraction for a minute and a half, then it would let up for fifteen seconds, and then it would start up again for another minute and a half. This was how it was going. I was throwing up the entire time. I was telling my husband, "Honey, just kill me, please kill me!" Then I started telling him where he could stick it, and then I told him to go find a new wife. Any woman who has had a baby will understand.

I started pushing. Three hours later I was still pushing, but by then I had lost all sense of reality. I was still puking and the pain was just getting worse and worse. This time it was not letting up. To add to the moment, the room was full of people, just crammed full of doctors, nurses and many others. Everybody was screaming. They pushed my husband off to the side and put oxygen on me. The pain was getting so bad that I told my husband, "I'm going to die," but he didn't hear me.

They were screaming, "Get her down to the O.R.!" I looked over at the monitor, and the baby's heart was beating 40 beats per minute. Babies are supposed to be at 160-170 beats a minute, so I knew we were in trouble. At that point my concern was for the baby. I had gone into what is called pre-rupture syndrome, a contraction that starts and doesn't let up. When that happens, the baby doesn't get any oxygen, you rupture, then both of you die.

I was still coherent enough to realize that was probably what was happening. It's horrible knowing too much. I knew I was going to die because I was rupturing and I could tell that the baby was probably already dead. In my fogged-in brain I knew these things were happening. And the pain was so bad!

We got into the operating room, and they put me up in stirrups because they were going to try forceps to pull the baby out. They hooked the fetal heart monitor back up, put me up in the stirrups and were getting the forceps out. All of a sudden I looked over, and I could hear the tone of the heartbeat going down even further. It went to 40 and then to 30, and the nurse said, "We've lost the baby!" The doctors that were there yelled for the neo-natal resuscitation team. My doctor looked at me and said, "The baby's dead." I looked at him and thought, "That's not all that's going to be dead." I was so angry.

I noticed that my pressure was down to 50 and I

knew what was next. I just kept thinking, "Thank goodness! I'll be dead in about two minutes and I won't have to go through this pain any more!"

The doctor said, "Forget the forceps, let's cut her." They threw my legs down out of the stirrups and somebody took some betadone and dumped it on my stomach. Nobody was talking to me. I pulled the mask off my face and looked at the anesthesiologist and I said, "I want you to tell my husband I love him." They never did. Instead they said, "It's going to be fine Mrs. M." I wanted to tell them off, because I knew what was happening.

He put the mask back on, and the doctor yelled to get a bed up in the ICU for me, and then he said, "Is she out? I gotta cut, I gotta go! Is she out?" The anesthesiologist said, "No. Wait a minute!"

About then I heard this buzz starting in my head, just a buzz. The anesthesiologist said, "I have to give her the medicine, wait a minute!" I thought to myself, "You don't need to worry about it. I'm dying." I looked up to the monitor where I could see my pressure falling. Above all the noise I could hear them yelling, "We're losing her!" And then the doctor yelled to get the code team down there now, the adult one.

I don't know what else they did, but the next
thing I knew I was standing next to my body, half in
and half out. I didn't go up to the ceiling. I was just
partially standing in the shoulder area of my body. I
felt them putting the breathing tube in, and I felt the
doctor cutting my abdomen open, but there was no
pain. Just like that! There was no pain. It was like a
breath of fresh air.

I just sat there taking it all in for a minute. It
was really white, almost foggy white, but it was really
clear in the center. Off in the periphery it was really
hazy where the white blended in. There were no walls
or definition, yet I could see the room. I could see the
stands holding all the instruments. I could see some
machinery off in the corner. I could see the baby bed
warmer, and yet it was all in a mist.

And then all of a sudden I realized— I had died!
It was a pretty big relief actually, because the pain had
been so bad. Then I realized that the light which was
illuminating everything was coming from behind me,
and a voice said to my mind, "It's okay if you want to
come home now, but there's more for you to do."

It was my choice. It was a hard choice. I knew
if I went back it would be hard and that it would even
get harder. It felt so good not having any more pain.

It was such a relief, it was so peaceful and comforting. But, I knew if I turned around I would see this person and I wouldn't want to go back. I didn't dare turn around. I knew enough by then to know exactly who it was and what was going on. I knew if I turned around and looked him in the eye I wouldn't come back, and yet I knew I had to come back. I knew whatever that work was that I had promised to do, I had to complete it.

I am convinced now that there must have been more to it than what I can recall, but that's all I remember. At that moment everything went black. A little later this nurse said to me, "Mrs. M., you have a new baby boy!" In my head I thought, "I already know that." I knew that I was still unconscious and in a coma, but in my head I was very much aware of what was going on, and I knew I had a baby boy. How could I have known? I had to have been told. But I don't recall being told.

Since the experience there have been things that have happened that I knew, but that I couldn't exactly recall. I think the rest of my experience has been blocked from my memory in order to test me. If I could remember everything I would make all the right decisions, but now I have to rely more on faith.

It is very frustrating, however, knowing that I have seen things or know of things to come, but that I don't recognize it until it has already happened.

I never could get a hold of my medical records to see if I had actually died. They wouldn't let me look at them. I think I was unconscious for about eight or twelve hours. I don't know if my heart actually stopped, or if it just got close. I know that two days later when they tried to sit me up for the first time, I kept passing out. I finally went home two weeks later.

They never would tell me what happened. They just put me off. I told the anesthesiologist, "You know, when you put me to sleep, you didn't put me to sleep, and I want to know what happened." He just looked at me really strange and said, "I can't discuss this," and he walked out of the room. I asked the surgeon, I asked the nurses, but they wouldn't tell me if they coded me. They didn't tell me if they coded my child. To this day I have no idea what happened to me while I was on the table.

I look back on it now, and I realize it was hell, but I needed to go through it to appreciate the good things. Unless you've gone through your own personal hell, you'll never be able to appreciate the good, and the peace and the beauty of heaven. You will not be contented with it. I look back on it and realize it was all very purposeful. It prepared me for completing my mission. It is a mission that is coming from inside.

Janet M.

CHAPTER TEN

HE CALLED ME BOBBY ANN

It was a December Wednesday, an average
workday morning, 1976. I was on my way to
work. I remember thinking of all the things I had to do
that day, hoping everything would fit together so I
could get them all done.

I was an educational consultant with several
meetings and inservice appointments planned with
teachers that day. I was reviewing all this in my mind
when a car pulled out in front of me. I was on a four
lane highway traveling in the left-hand lane.

It was a cloudy morning with patches of fog set-
tling on the road, resulting in slippery spots. Seeing
the car pull in front of me, I hit the brakes. My car
began spinning, turning around in the road, crossing
the opposing lanes of traffic, sliding into a field and
striking an old cement foundation which caused the

car to roll into a tree.

For a moment, after hitting the foundation, it seemed I was above the car, watching it roll across the field into the tree. Then everything was quiet. Maybe I was unconscious, at least catching my breath.

When I regained my senses, I knew I was trapped in the car, prone on my back. It didn't appear there was much damage from my position under the dash. I remember thinking it strange that the windshield wasn't even broken. Later I learned the car was totally demolished and the windshield broken into a thousand pieces. When I tried to move, I couldn't.

I decided I had to let people know I was there, knowing I was quite a distance from the road. I started honking the horn as best I could. I picked a rhythm so those hearing it would know the honking was deliberate, not just a stuck horn.

Eventually a young man came to the car, looked down and shook his head. I gave him the phone numbers of my work place and my husband's work place, and asked him to please call. He just shook his head and left. I wasn't sure if he was going to make the calls so I started blowing the horn again.

A few minutes later I looked up and saw people I knew, plus a state policeman. They were looking down at me rather strangely. I didn't know why they were looking that way. I suppose it might have been the incoherent way I was talking. I asked the officer to please be sure there was no mention of the accident in the newspaper.

Soon an ambulance came. A young man and woman pulled me out of the car. They said they thought my legs were hurt. I found out later my thigh bone was broken, as was my pelvis in three places. The ball joint had been pushed right through the socket. Three ribs on my left side were broken too. There were particles of glass in my face, a collapsed lung, ruptured spleen, and internal bleeding so profuse that later in the hospital I went through 30 pints of blood during two operations.

I remember the ambulance ride to the hospital, and being taken into emergency, where I waited from 9 a.m. until 5 p.m. for a surgeon to become available to operate. In the meantime they began cleaning up my face, removing mostly small chunks of glass from my mouth and skin. They began giving me fluids through a needle in my arm.

I remember looking up at a doctor who had sweat on his face as he called for another doctor. He was calling for a surgeon. He knew I was bleeding internally and had broken bones.

I remember wishing it would hurt more so I could pass out and not have to experience everything that was going on. For a while I seemed to be going in and out of consciousness. I couldn't talk or express myself, but I seemed to hear everything that was going on. I remember the following conversation between two of the people working on me.

"She came in in pretty bad shape, and if we don't get busy she'll go out in a canvas bag," said one voice.

"Let's get busy," said another voice.

I was reminded of when I was a little girl watching my uncles catch and clean fish. I could hear the same kinds of sounds, as when my uncles cut open and cleaned their fish. I didn't know what the doctors were doing to me.

It was quiet, or blank, for a while, then I heard a voice say, "What's her blood pressure?" "Thirty over zero," was the reply.

"Come on you fools," I remember thinking. "Those numbers are not blood pressure readings. They may have something to do with the weather outside, but not my blood pressure."

"We better get moving on this," a voice said. "If

we don't, we'll lose her."

The next thing I remember is sliding down a trough or slide. At a certain point I remember being very reluctant, feeling cold. There was a strange sound, not quite like a siren or whistle, but very loud and unlike any sound I had ever heard before.

When I got to the bottom of the slide I was suddenly warm. My surroundings were beautiful, like a garden—with flowers, lawn, trees, etc. It reminded me of a park by the river where I had gone as a child for family reunions. There were people visiting and walking about.

I saw my father sitting on one of the benches. I went over to him. I remember communicating with him. I don't say talking, because I don't remember hearing any sounds.

"Daddy, please let me stay," I asked. "Please let me stay. I don't want to go back. It will hurt too much. I don't want to go through all that. I just want to stay here."

I could feel the peace and beauty of the place. The people were calm and happy. It was kind of like a college campus. I could feel a warm, accepting atmosphere.

My father was shaking his head and looking at

me, not saying anything. Then my grandmother appeared, telling me I couldn't stay. She said I had to go back, that I wasn't finished yet. I told her I didn't want to go back, that I wanted to stay. Yet, somehow I knew she had the final word. She had always been a forceful, authoritative person, who believed you did the things that were hard to do because they were right. I knew I had to go back.

My father looked just like he had looked the last time I saw him, pretty much in the prime of his life, calm and in control. Grandmother looked harassed and harried, kind of tense. I remember her being that way before she died. I got the feeling that she wasn't at as high a level of spiritual development as my father was. She had come from a different part of the afterworld, from a group of people who were unsettled like she was, less distinct in their appearance, and not as much in control as my father. He was benign and calm, like he had been in life.

Though I don't remember this part, one of my friends who visited me immediately following the surgery said I told her I had visited with my father who had called me by the nick name that only he called me, Bobby Ann. She said I told her that my father said I had to go back because I had other work to do. When I asked him what the work was, his only response was that I would know. That was all he could say at that time.

After the discussions with my father and grandmother, the next thing I remember was waking up in my hospital bed and looking into the faces of relatives. The orthopedic physician who operated on me came in one day and said, "I can't forget who you are. You are the one who went to the other side. Everything shut down. You had no vital signs. Do you know who was in the Jesus seat?"

"No."

"The anesthesiologist. He brought you back."

I wanted to disagree with him, tell him that it was my father and grandmother who made me come back, but instead I said nothing, figuring he probably wouldn't understand my near death experience.

Barbara R.

CHAPTER ELEVEN

MY FUTURE CHILDREN WERE IN THE TUNNEL

My husband Dave was in a graduate school of engineering in the late sixties. We had two little girls, and I was pregnant with our third child.

One Sunday evening I began hemorrhaging, a little at first, but then it became serious. Dave had to keep bringing me fresh towels as the old ones became soggy with blood. He ran to the nearest pay phone to call the doctor who wasn't in, but the lady taking the calls told Dave to give me paregoric.

The bleeding continued until we decided we had better go to the hospital. When I tried to get out of bed I passed out, collapsing onto the floor. Dave dragged me into the kitchen. I remember feeling cold, but calm as Dave tried to revive me.

About this time my sister stopped by. She was on her way home and wanted to see how I was doing. Upon seeing me on the kitchen floor, she screamed. She sent Dave to get a registered nurse who lived across the street. While at the nurse's house, he called for an ambulance.

The nurse could see by the way my eyes were dilating that I was going into shock. She wrapped me in blankets. By the time the ambulance arrived, I was feeling much better, though I still felt cold.

The doctor met me at the hospital. At first our conversation was casual.

"What have you been doing?" he asked. "Bleeding all over the house, " I responded.

I suppose he didn't take me serious, because it wasn't until the nurse took my blood pressure that he became very earnest.

"You didn't tell me you were bleeding," he shouted. "We've got to go into surgery immediately."

He began swearing when he discovered the lights were off and the door locked in surgery. It was late.

Twenty minutes later I found myself on the

operating table. Because of my low blood level, I was informed I would not be receiving any anesthetic. The doctor was preparing to perform a dilation and curerage (D&C).

I remember how painful it was as the doctor went to work. For the first time I felt terror. I was afraid to die. The next thing I remember was the voice of the nurse.

"Doctor, her breathing has stopped," she said.

"Doctor, her pulse is gone," she added.

I felt my spirit kind of gathering to the middle of my body, then draining out the back. I found myself in the corner of the room, floating in mid-air, watching the doctor and nurses trying to revive the body on the operating table.

I felt like I could go back to my body but didn't want to. Suddenly I was aware of a dark tunnel, like a doorway leaving the operating room. I could see it, but the doctor and nurses couldn't. Though I was afraid, I entered the tunnel and found myself traveling very fast towards the far end. I wasn't walking or running, just floating along, very fast. There was a light at the end of the tunnel. It wasn't a blue light, but a warm golden light, very bright. As I neared the end of the tunnel it became very narrow, but I made it through, finding myself in an open place with other people. I recognized two of them, my grandfather, Leo Bowers whom I had known as a little girl, and my great-grandfather, Richard Britton. Both of them were very glad to see me.

The glowing personage who had been the light at the end of the tunnel told me I had to go back. He said no one else could raise my little girls for me. He said my life would be hard, but he would be with me. This communication didn't seem to be with words. Thoughts just passed back and forth.

Somehow I felt cheated that I was not being allowed to stay with the rest of the people around me. I still didn't want to go back.

The next thing I remember was the doctor hitting me in the face, very hard.

"Listen to me," he said, forcefully. "You are not leaving this room as long as I am here."

The next day he told me the reason he had struck me and spoken so forcefully was because he could see that I was gone, and he sensed that I didn't want to come back.

On several occasions I tried to tell people what

had happened, but I was rebuffed. They thought I had been hallucinating, or that the loss of blood had caused brain damage. Even my husband didn't want me to tell anyone what had happened.

As a result, I kept the experience to myself for many years, though I continued to think a lot about what had happened. I became obsessed with the meaning of life and experiencing the most life could offer. I began reading a lot. I remembered the messenger's promise that he would be with me. Though I have never seen his face again or heard his voice, I have felt that same quiet, confident communication when I have been seeking solutions to life's difficult problems.

Against the doctors' advice, I became pregnant four more times, losing two of the babies prematurely, and coming near death again with another of the pregnancies. I knew that several of the people I had seen at the end of the tunnel were to be my future children, so I continued getting pregnant until I felt I had brought them into the world. Now I am no longer afraid of death.

Jean S.

CHAPTER TWELVE

PUSHED BACK INTO MY BODY

When I was a year old a tumor started growing on the left side of my face. It grew bigger and bigger until it was as large as a grapefruit, totally disfiguring my face. The doctors said I had neurofibromatosis, or elephant man's disease.

As I grew older I lost a leg to the disease, and by the time I was 22 the tumor was getting so large that it was only a matter of time before it would cut off my breathing. I was desperate. I knew I would die if the tumor was not removed.

Then I was examined by Dr. Bruce Leipzig at the University of Arkansas hospital in Little Rock. He said he thought the tumor might be isolated and hadn't grown through and around other tissue as most other doctors seemed to think. He was willing to do his best to remove it.

The surgery was scheduled, I was admitted to the hospital and the operation was performed. The doctors said the operation was a success. The next day I felt good enough to want to go home. The doctors were surprised I felt so good. I had used fifteen pints of blood during the operation.

On the third day when Dr. Leipzig came in to see me I began to take a turn for the worse. He detected abnormal swelling in my face. He discovered blood clots and decided emergency surgery was needed.

I remember just before the operation kneeling on my hospital bed, pleading with the Lord to spare my life, promising that if I lived through the operation I would serve him the remainder of my life.

After my prayer, they wheeled me into the operating room. The doctors and aids strapped me to the operating table, flat on my back my arms extended straight out. One of my thoughts was how funny that an operating table is shaped much like a cross. I couldn't move, not even my head.

After applying some local anesthetic, they began inserting various life support tubes prior to putting me under. The doctor who was numbing my throat with a cotton swab continued to apologize for the discomfort he was causing me. A laryngoscope was pushed down my throat to keep the passageway open and clear for a tube which went into my lungs. The general anesthetic couldn't be applied until all the life support tubes were in place.

While all this was happening I suddenly passed out. The next thing I remember was being able to sit up. This was both surprising and confusing to me because I remembered how tightly the doctors had strapped me down. Yet, I was sitting up, easily and comfortably. In fact, all the pain and discomfort were suddenly gone. I had a feeling of overwhelming peace. The trauma and stress were gone. It was like I was standing beside a clear blue lake under an apple tree on a beautiful summer day, a cool breeze blowing in my face.

I could see the doctors, standing around me, doing their various jobs. But I could see other people too. They were dressed in white robes. The material the robes were made from was not like silk or satin, but more substantial, like tweed or homespun.

I was filled with a feeling of total peace. All the fear I had felt earlier was gone. For the first time in years my body was totally free of pain. I realized I was dying, and I was happy. I had no desire to go back.

I was in transition between the physical world

and the spirit world. I was halfway between two plains of existence, and could see both. There was a kind of greenish hue to the physical world where the doctors worked on me. The spirit world was more subdued in color, not bright at all.

I don't know how much time passed while all this was taking place. It seemed to me like a long time, but in the physical world it may have only been a few seconds. I don't know.

Eventually one of the men in white robes came up to me. The fact that my legs were strapped out in front of me on the operating table didn't seem to hinder his ability to stand directly in front of me. As he drew near I felt an overwhelming love radiating from him. I could not see his face, but I could feel how much he cared for me. He reached forward—I could see his arms—and placed his hands on my upper arms.

Though I could not hear words, the message he had for me came clearly into my mind. It was not time for me to go. I still had a lot to do in the physical world.

Though I didn't want to go back, the being in front of me pushed me gently, but firmly, back into my body. I didn't resist his power. I had a great desire to please this man and return to my life here.

The next thing I remember was waking up in my room. I spent two more weeks in the hospital and another six weeks recovering at home. During that time I was in kind of a haze, with a weird, detached feeling, almost like part of my spirit was not in my body, but that feeling gradually went away.

The operation was a success. The tumor has not returned, though I am still undergoing reconstructive surgery. Sometimes life is still hard, but it is good. I am grateful to the man in the white robe who pushed me back into my body.

Marc S.

CHAPTER THIRTEEN

HIGHWAY 54 TO KANSAS, 1963

My experience occurred in 1963 when I was in a car accident. About four years before the accident I had begun studying for the Protestant Ministry. One reason was so that I could be of service to others, but another reason was simply that I was one of those persistent seekers after truth. I wanted to find more answers than I had found in high school and in college.

When the accident happened I was right in the middle of my freshman year in college. Before that particular time I had been really concerned because I wasn't finding the answers I was looking for. School was meaning less and less to me. In fact, I even intuitively told my roommate that I probably wouldn't be back after Christmas, not knowing what I was talking about at all.

I was very frustrated. The dean of students even told me that I should—unlike other students—study less and relax more, and not try so hard. With that advice I backed off a little bit, but it still didn't make me happy. After I told my roommate I might not be back after Christmas, I had a feeling to tell him that something was going to happen to me, not that I wasn't going to be enrolled again, but that something serious was going to happen. Several weeks before that, when I was praying, I asked God if he would have something happen in my life that would kind of wake me up and get me started in the right direction. I had no idea where to turn for answers.

I went home to California by train from Kansas, where I was going to school, and had a normal Christmas vacation. Our neighbor across the street was driving back to Illinois to go to some kind of graduate school with the Air Force. He needed somebody to go with him to help him stay awake during the long drive. It would take about two days of straight driving to go from California to Illinois. On the way we would go through Kansas where he would drop me off.

The really interesting thing was that in 1963 there was very little concern for seatbelts, and the ones that were in cars were lap belts only. My friend had gotten them for Christmas and had just installed them in his big Buick. We used the seatbelts and even talked about how many accidents happen because people fall asleep while driving.

On our trip we had one car problem after another. Finally after spending half of a day in Albuquerque getting the radiator fixed, we were on our way again. On this stretch of road we found ourselves in snowstorms between Albuquerque and Tucumcari. We were taking Highway 54 through the Oklahoma panhandle, a landscape that is as flat as a board.

I was able to help keep Jack awake, but I could not relieve him by taking a turn at driving since I didn't have a driver's license yet. At about five o'clock in the morning we had to stop so he could get some coffee to keep awake.

When we got back on the road I remember the sun just starting to shed some light on the horizon. Then I saw headlights on our side of the two lane highway coming towards us. I asked Jack, "What is that car doing on our side of the highway?" He braked and got as far on to the shoulder as he could, and that is the last thing I remember. We hit head on, even though I don't remember the impact.

At that time I didn't feel any pain at all, I felt

kind of euphoric, and optimistic, like everything was okay. I don't think that I was having any kind of out-of-the-body-experience at that time. I just know that I didn't feel bad. I was probably in shock.

The seatbelts kept me from going through the windshield, but I still hit my face on the dashboard, which fortunately was padded. Even so, I broke seventeen bones in my face. The combined 110 mph impact of the two big Buicks hitting each other was such a stress that the seatbelt crushed my innards and fractured my spinal column without even breaking the skin. The seatbelt saved my life, even though it caused me some serious injuries. Jack was in pretty bad shape as well because the steering wheel had gone into his chest.

I don't know how long it was before an emergency vehicle finally showed up to get us out of the car. We were both taken to Guymon Memorial Hospital. This was about the coldest it had been in the Oklahoma panhandle in years, and the hospital was full of people with pneumonia. There were even beds out in the hallways. I remember they had taken me in, and I was awake long enough to realize that they were cutting off my new shirt that I had just gotten for Christmas. There was blood all over me which

indicated that I had lost a lot. The nurses were scurry-
ing around trying to find AB blood. They were desperately trying to save my life.

A lot of people that have had life after death
experiences can remember quite a bit of detail. I don't
remember much detail. I don't remember a tunnel, but
I do remember a light, and I remember the intensity of
everything that I saw. I remember that nobody talked
to me. It was like we didn't need to talk. We would
just read each other's minds in a form of immediate
communication. I felt very peaceful, and I felt a lot of
love. Then there was this being. Ever since my experience I have been trying, even praying about it, to get
personal revelation to see whether he was my grandfather who had passed away six months before. He had
been kind of my mentor, in a sense, because he had
been interested in religion and had done a lot of
preaching as a substitute pastor in his ministry at
home. I have never felt that it was Jesus Christ, but I
haven't been able to completely convince myself of
who it was. My parents weren't dead, so my grandfather was the most immediate relative back in my
ancestry to give me life, so that's why I still have a
very strong sense that it was my grandfather. Even so,
I just know it was a being who loved me very much.

I probably saw him and recognized him, but like
so many other things, I don't remember. It was like
there was an additional veil drawn over my memory.
In comparing my experience with those of others it
seems like we get the understanding and insight we
need for our lives; some people need more, and some
people need less.

In any case, I was given the golden question of
whether I wanted to stay or whether I wanted to go
back to my body. Of course, I saw how beautiful it
was. The colors were so intense. The light was kind
of golden, and the green was very intense. It wasn't
fluorescent green. It was just really, really intense. It
was like I could almost see the life in the leaves. I felt
like I could see the spirit as well as the substance of
the leaves.

I wish I could remember more. Sometimes in a
dream I will remember more, but the last memory
that came back to me in a dream was the impact of
the head on collision, and that was just a couple of
years ago. I guess it was time for that to come out. It
was very frightening, but I was able to gain a better
sense of what the impact was like and what it did to
my body.

While I was with the being who I think was my

grandfather, I could also sense the presence of other people around, although I don't remember seeing them. This being then asked me which direction I would take. "Now look," he said, "this is what you get if you stay here, but there are worlds even better than this, and if you stay here now, you may or may not be able to experience those other worlds because you haven't yet found the truth. But, on the other hand, if you decide to go back into your body you are going to find the truth. It's going to be a long struggle. You're not going to find it right away, and it's going to be very discouraging for you. The other thing that's going to happen to you is that because you've had this experience, you're going to go through more in your life than most people do." It was clear to me that I would be able to do that, because I had a perfect knowledge that there is a life after death. I'm not afraid to die. I'm ready to go anytime—that's probably why I'll live a long time! Sometimes when life gets discouraging I even think "Well, is it maybe time now?" Anyway, obviously I took the second choice and came back.

I remember feeling good about the choice, but of course, almost immediately I was immersed in pain. The pain continued for a while, but I knew that I had to get through this, and I started healing very rapidly. My doctor had told me that I probably would never walk again since my back had been so badly damaged. He said the lumbar region in my back was just like mashed potatoes. Later he told me, "Yours is the most miraculous recovery I've ever seen in all my years of practice."

They thought it would take me about six months to recover, but in about two and a half months I had recovered to the point where they could fit me with a back brace, and send me home to California. It was not too long after that that I was able to get around on my own. Now I live as normal a life as anyone, and for that I am extremely grateful.

Gary G.

CHAPTER FOURTEEN

I SAW MY FIRST WIFE

My first wife, Carol, always said logging was a good way to get killed. But when I was out of work the summer of 1987, it seemed like the best way to provide for my family.

Years earlier I was in the army. I had been commissioned as a chaplain and was stationed at Fort Sill, Oklahoma with Carol and our four children. When the mother of Carol's friend died from breast cancer, Carol became concerned about some soreness she had been experiencing. She had it checked. They found a malignant tumor so large the doctors gave us little hope. Carol went through the mastectomy, the chemo-therapy and the radiation treatments, but died in December of 1984.

I've always felt that Carol was somehow instrumental in my meeting and marrying Crystal. Crystal moved into our neighborhood with her four girls after Carol and I left for Fort Sill. Following Carol's death, Crystal and I were introduced. We were married a short time later.

My older brother, Mike, had done more logging than me and helped purchase a nice stand of trees in the Payette National Forest. The trees averaged six thousand pounds, were sixty to seventy feet tall and eighteen to twenty-four inches in diameter.

Mike and I and a friend, Art, were logging the stand on May 22, 1987. About 11:30 a.m., Art came over to where I was and asked for help on a tree. He had wedged it on the back cut trying to get it to fall uphill, but it had bound up his saw.

When I examined the tree a little more closely, I found a pitch seam on the uphill side. That usually indicated the tree was unsound and could split, creating what we called a "barber chair". If the tree splits as it falls, it will sometimes kick the base of the tree out from the stump leaving a slab on the stump resembling a high back barber chair. It is a very dangerous situation.

I told Art to start cutting with my saw. When the tree started falling, he was to run along the slope of the hill perpendicular to the fall of the tree. I would pull his saw out as soon as it became loose and run the other way.

The tree split as I suspected. Art ran, I got the chain saw out, dropped it and ran in the opposite direction. The tree, however, did not fall exactly as we had expected. As we measured later, I was twent-eight feet from the stump when the tree split and bar-ber-chaired. The base of the tree trunk, sharpened by the chainsaw cuts, leaped from the stump in my direc-tion spearing me in the back at shoulder height. I felt my back snap as I was driven into the ground face-first, filling my mouth and eyes full of dirt. The tree trunk then slammed down on top of me.

As the weight of the tree crushed down on me, I felt my spirit leave my body. I knew immediately I was dead. There was no question. It was all over.

The first emotion I felt was terror. I did not want it to be over. I wanted to be with my wife and kids. I had things to do, things to accomplish. The terror was soon replaced by disappointment.

When I was in high school I was starting line-man on our undefeated football team. I've thought the disappointment I felt at the accident was probably like being pulled out of a championship football game, put on the sidelines and told I was through playing. For the rest of the game I had to watch. I did not want to watch, I wanted to play. I wanted to be in the action.

Following the accident I felt a great acceleration of speed like I was traveling very fast through the darkness that had now closed in around me. I also noticed that my mind was very alert and crystal clear. I could comprehend anything. I was not constrained by my body. I noticed that the pain was completely gone, and I had no discomfort at all.

The earlier fear and disappointment were replaced by peace and a definite feeling of well-being. Everything was okay. Everything was just as it should be. As this feeling came, I emerged out of the darkness and became aware that I was not alone. I felt the presence of people before I actually saw anyone.

As I looked, I saw my first wife, Carol, my mother who had died in 1974 from a stroke, and my Grandfather who had died in 1974. He had been in his late eighties or early nineties when he died.

Being reunited with my loved ones, especially my first wife filled me with the greatest feelings of love, acceptance and overwhelming sweetness.

We began conversing, but not with words. Communication was total and absolute and seemed to be pure thoughts communicated from mind to mind. There was no possibility of misunderstanding.

They had come to meet me and escort me to the spirit world–if I chose to go. They told me that I had a choice. I could stay or go. They did not try at all to persuade me one way or the other, but expressed concern for Crystal and the kids if I decided not to return.

Carol was not jealous of Crystal at all. There was not the least bit of pettiness, envy or resentment. In fact, she stated that she was pleased that we had gotten married and was very concerned for Crystal's well-being if I left.

I was overjoyed to see her and bask in her love and warmth and was not eager to be separated again. She told me not to worry about our separation, that time was not the same in the spirit world. She said life was very short, that I should return and complete my responsibilities to Crystal and the children, and then we would be together again.

Grandad had white hair but appeared to be in his early forties. Mom was in her late twenties or early thirties like I remembered her when I was very young. Carol was as I remembered her in her middle to late twenties. She had brown hair. All of them wore loose-fitting, white robes. Mom's and Carol's robes were the same basic design, though slightly different.

When I emerged out of the darkness and was met by Carol, Mom, and Grandad, I noticed that we were at the scene of the accident, standing in the air above the ground about ceiling height. I could see Art sawing the tree to get the weight off of me. Then I saw him check for pulse and respiration. He thought I was dead and ran to get Mike who was working about a half-mile away. This, however, was not the focus of my attention. I was much more involved in the sweet reunion with loved ones and not concerned with what was going on below.

I remember expressing concern over being crippled. I knew what I had felt when the tree hit me, and I could see my body underneath the tree. I did not want to have the test of a handicap for the rest of my life. I felt that was probably one test I couldn't handle. They knew my thoughts and told me that if I chose to return, my body would be okay. I then agreed to go back if my body would recover. I don't remember any farewells or goodbyes. The next thing I remember I was back in my body. I immediately wiggled my toes and fingers to make sure I was not paralyzed. It hurt so badly, though, that I didn't try to do it again.

Mike and Crystal have told me things I said by the tree and at the hospital that I can't remember. It makes me think that more went on than I recall. I know I can't be sure where certain impressions came from. When Art and Mike returned, the first thing I said was that I needed to sell the motorcycle or Aaron, my oldest son, was going to kill himself on it. This thought had not occurred to me before. In fact, I had just fixed it to get it in good shape.

Mike was a trained Emergency Medical Technician and made sure I didn't try to move until he checked me out thoroughly. While he was doing that, he asked me if I had been in communication with Carol, Mom and Grandad. I said I had, but I wanted to know why he had asked. He explained that when he came to the scene, he had felt their presence. I thought it peculiar that he would mention all three.

Mike and Art spent another hour clearing a space in the trees for the pickup so I could be loaded and taken to the hospital. While they were doing that, I was sliding in and out of consciousness. I did not think about what had happened to me. I was just trying to cope with the pain and hang on. It wasn't until the last day in the hospital and the first days at home that I was able to recall my out-of-body experience and sort things out.

When I arrived at the hospital, they were immediately concerned about internal injuries. They found that my shoulder blade was broken into six pieces, my hip had been out of socket, and I had broken one of the small bones that proceeds laterally from the vertebrae. My back felt like jelly.

The doctors couldn't imagine why the force of the tree trunk, which was great enough to shatter my shoulder blade, had not crushed my back and ribs. They were also surprised that the sharpened, jagged base of the tree had not broken any skin. My clothes were torn slightly, but there was no blood anywhere.

As I had time to think about what happened, more details became clear to me. I've felt what it is to feel and enjoy the love of God. I learned that the other side is organized by families. I also received the strong impression that positions at work, in society or in churches are not important at all. What matters is how we treat people, whether or not we are kind to them and what kind of relationships we build with our families. All of these things were conveyed to me when a falling tree enabled me to pass to the other side.

Kent J.

CHAPTER FIFTEEN

STRANGERS EMBRACED ME

When I was about seven years old I had a playmate named Dennis. He lived next door to us in Edgbaston, Warwick, England. Dennis' mother died that year. It was customary in England at that time for close friends and relatives to pay last respects at the home before the body was taken to the funeral parlor.

I remember my mother going next door to see Dennis' mother for the last time. I was not allowed to go because I was too young.

When mother returned she was sad and upset. I tried to comfort her by saying, "I'm sure she was happy that you came. I wish I could have gone with you."

My comment only made my mother angry. "She couldn't have been happy, or sad, or anything else," Mother replied. "She is dead. Her life is over, finished."

"When someone dies they can still hear and see, just not respond," I argued. I don't know where the idea came from, only that I had not been taught that at home.

"Absolutely not," Mother insisted. "When you die your life comes to an end. You are no more."

I was a child and she was an adult so, of course, she won the argument. As a result I became very much afraid of death, especially two years later, at age nine, when I became seriously ill with pluerisy and double pneumonia. I had had many illnesses as a child. I received all the medication available, but still did not get well.

The doctor visited our home one evening and after examining me, told my mother, as I found out later, that I would probably not live through the night, that my death could come at any moment. He told her to make me as comfortable as possible, and recommended extra hot water bottles on my chest and along my sides.

About an hour after the doctor's departure, the pain became even more intense, so my mother decided to go next door to fetch another hot water bottle.

Though I hadn't heard what the doctor had said, I was crying that I didn't want to die. I was afraid to die. I was terrified. My mother tried to comfort me, telling me I was not going to die. I remember continuing to cry as she went next door to borrow the hot water bottle.

Shortly after Mother left the room, the pain became unbearable. Even crying brought agony. I remember for a few seconds trying to catch my breath, then suddenly the pain was gone, completely.

At first I thought I might have fallen asleep. Then I realized I was looking down on myself in my bed. I could see the entire house, in front of the house, and my mother in the house next door talking to the neighbor. I felt so peaceful and good.

Then I was aware that I was not alone. People were gathering around me, and welcoming me. I felt surrounded by so much love. They were dressed in white and some of them embraced me. I felt so happy. I didn't know who the people were, but I felt like I knew them and they knew me. Together we began moving towards a white light.

"No, no, she has to go back," said a voice, stopping our progress towards the light.

"No, I don't want to go back," I protested.

"You must return."

The voice was strong, but not loud, the kind of voice you don't argue with. Three times it told me I must return.

I could see my body again, in the bedroom. I saw my mother return from the neighbors, climb the stairs, and go over to me on the bed. She took my hand, presumably to check my pulse. Then she dropped my arm back on the bed. She turned briefly toward the window.

My bedroom window had been open, and when she had noticed from the neighbors that I had stopped crying, she had hurried home. Unable to feel my pulse, she turned towards the window to gather her strength.

Suddenly all the pain was back again, and I was hurting and crying. Mother hurried back to my bed.

As I became well I did not tell anyone about my experience. In fact I kept it to myself for many years, fearing ridicule, not wanting people to think I was crazy. Yet I could not forget that experience and the wonderful feelings of love and peace I experienced for just a short while. I knew my spirit had left my body for a short while, then returned again.

Doreen E.

CHAPTER SIXTEEN
AL-CAN HIGHWAY, 1976

The weather during August 1976 was hot and humid just south of the border between Alaska and the Yukon. My husband, our five children and I were heading back to the States after a tiring and disappointing job-hunting trip to Alaska. We were taking turns driving the four-wheel drive van Tom had recently acquired for our venture.

The night before we left Alaska, it had rained, and once we left the pavement of the Alaskan highways and re-entered Canada, the rutted road of the unpaved Al-Can Highway became muddy. Tom and I had traded places, and I was driving while the rest of the family slept. I was handling the unfamiliar vehicle fairly well when I came to a stretch of road that had been freshly oiled to keep down the dust during the dry spells. Even though my speed was just under ten miles an hour, I could feel the van's tires slip from time to time. I slowed down to a crawl, but pools of water from the recent rain had settled on top of the oiled road and formed a continuous, greasy, mud slick.

Suddenly, the van began to slide. I struggled to get it under control and had just managed to do so when I felt the tires slide on another greasy section of road. I knew we were going to go over the embankment, and there was nothing I could do to stop us.

I remember screaming for my husband to wake up. Then we were over the side and rolling down the slope with children screaming and luggage flying everywhere. I remember being pulled outside my body where I watched the entire event from afar. I felt as if I was being pulled backward down a long tube. I could see everything happening from a distance. It was very clear although it looked small, as if I was seeing everything from the wrong end of a telescope. I felt myself totally surrounded by others who gave me a strong feeling of support and concern for my well being. I did not turn to look at these beings, though I somehow knew how they looked. Instead, I demanded of them, "Am I dead? Am I dead?" Instantly, I knew I was alive, and at that moment, I snapped back into my body and found myself in the midst of turmoil.

Everyone had survived, including a rather

stunned me, but I have never forgotten that I almost moved on to the other side that day. There was no fear there; rather, there was a sense of support and encouragement from those waiting to help me on my way. Coming back gave me a shock and made me feel a sense of loss that I have never forgotten.

Barbara J. H.

CHAPTER SEVENTEEN

SOME KIND OF MISTAKE

In July of 1976, about four or five in the after-noon, my heart attack began. I was loading short railroad ties into the back of my pickup on some property where we ran cattle twenty miles up Spanish Fork Canyon, east of Spanish Fork, Utah. I was about 17 miles from my home in Mapleton.

The attack began with sharp pains behind both of my collar bones, just below the base of the neck. After four or five minutes my chest felt like it was being squeezed, under some kind of pressure.

I decided to drive up to my ranch where I could lie on the grass under the shade of a tree until the pain and discomfort went away. It hadn't yet occurred to me that I was having a heart attack.

I was driving towards the ranch when some-thing told me I had better get out of the canyon while

I still could. Upon reaching the highway, instead of turning towards the ranch, I headed straight for home.

I hadn't gone more than a block when I felt a numbness pouring from the neck and chest area into my arms. It was a smooth sensation, like someone pouring water. At the same time I felt the numbness moving up my neck into my head. The fight was on to see if I could make it home.

I told myself I wasn't going to go any faster than forty miles per hour in the event I got in an accident. I set the speed control at 40 mph so I could forget about keeping my foot on the accelerator.

I began to black out, at least partially. I kept repeating to myself that if I could just make the straight-away east of Thistle I would be all right. When I made that I told myself if I could make it to Thistle Rock I would be okay. Next it was to the old D.O.L. gas station, and then to Castilla Hot Springs. Meanwhile, my head was becoming increasingly fuzzy.

By the time I reached the Covered Bridge Canyon turnoff I was mostly unconscious. I decided I had better pull off the road before I hurt someone. This was before the road was widened, so I had nowhere to go but off the oil onto the sloping shoulder.

I got out of the truck and sat down on the ground by the right rear tire. I was trying desperately to find a position where the pain would be relieved. I tried stretching out on the ground, first on one side, then the other, then on my back, then over on my belly. I tried lying down with my head uphill, then downhill. I even stood up again.

Nothing seemed to help. The pain kept getting worse. By this time I had started passing out, but always regained consciousness.

Finally, I went around to the front of the truck and pulled myself up on my knees with the help of the bumper, and stood up.

"Lord," I said, "If I am going to die, and this is how it is going to happen, I am not afraid. I can't ask for favors because the life I have lived has not been as it should be."

"Mother, Dad," I said, continuing, "if you are there, answer and let me know. If I could talk to either one of you it would help me."

For the first time in my life I felt like I had come from an egg or from under a rock. There was no feeling of anything, no ties to Mother or Dad, or my lineage.

I was facing west across the river looking at the maples on the side of the hill. Suddenly I felt myself rising in the air above the truck, looking down. I ascended into the sky, looking west, but traveling east. All at once the road was gone. So were the railroad tracks. Where the highway and railroad tracks had been there were trees. It was as if I had gone back in time a hundred, or perhaps a thousand years. There were no signs of man.

"This can't be," I said to myself. "I have traveled this canyon for years. There's got to be a mark, a trail, or something."

Then as suddenly as I had left I was back in my body. The pain was bad. I crawled back to the right rear tire, tried to sit up, then passed out. Again I was out of my body, looking down at it. My feet were uphill towards the truck, my head downhill towards the gutter. I was on my left side. A fly was flying around my face. I wanted to slap at it.

Suddenly I began moving up the mountain, suspended in air, like I was flying Buck Rogers style. It seemed I was traveling 20 to 25 miles per hour. Each time I drifted into unconsciousness I was in a light fog.

The air smelled like fresh rain. The branches on

the trees were wet. I thought it strange that no leaves were on the trees. It was July, or was it?

As I was speeding up the mountain, I suddenly felt the presence of someone else. At the same time I was getting too close to the trees.

"Look out," I said, "we're going to crash and get hurt in those limbs." We plowed into the trees. I threw up my hands to protect my face, but I couldn't feel any of the limbs hitting me. Finally, I took my hands down as tree tops flashed by on both sides of me. Nothing seemed to hurt me.

Then I found myself in some kind of strange cubicle, or it seemed so because it was totally quiet and I couldn't feel the air against me as I ascended up the mountain. The space I was in was three steps in one direction and four in the other. I could see the surrounding countryside in all directions. It was as if I was in a different dimension or time zone. It seemed my space or cubicle was made of glass and closed in.

I was standing in the front, in the northeast corner, and it seemed someone else was in the southwest corner at the rear. I took a quick glance back to see who it was, but received the distinct impression that I wasn't supposed to look. I tried to strike up a conversation, but after two or three short attempts, I felt I wasn't supposed to do that either.

Earlier, it had been very painful to breathe. Now as I attempted to breathe, I realized all the pain was gone.

We were gliding up the mountain. Then all of a sudden, I was back in my body sitting by the right hind wheel of my pickup. The pain was terrible.

"Lord," I prayed. "I'm going to ask something, not for me but for my wife. She's been a good woman all her life. If she comes up here in the middle of the night looking for me, and sees my truck over here, and tries to turn around, she might get in an accident and hurt or kill herself. Or someone else might. So if it's at all possible I would like to get out of the canyon so she won't have to come looking for me."

As I sat there, I could hear cars passing on the highway. I could hear the wind blowing up the canyon. I remember thinking how quiet it was, then thinking how stupid I was to think that.

Then I was in the enclosure again, high above the mountains, traveling very fast. It seemed I was a mile or two above the ground. I remember thinking that if I could get lower I could see better. Then, like, a flash I was traveling about a half mile above the mountains.

As I traveled along I remember seeing a light at the end of a large hole, which looked something like an irrigation culvert, but much bigger. I was being sucked towards it, and thought I was going to enter it—an endless vastness of forever.

I was almost into the tunnel when it suddenly disappeared, and I found myself in a bluish blackness. Everything around me was bluish black. It was like I was in a river. If I could get to the bank I could grab onto something, but there was nothing to grab onto. I was moving along. In the distance I could see a light, similar to about an eighth moon, upside down. It was a long way away. I had the strangest sensation, like my flesh was disintegrating and falling off my upper arms, then all over. It seemed my very being was discharging into nothingness. I was back in my body, coming back and forth between consciousness and unconsciousness.

Once in a while I could smell the moist, damp air, and feel the water dripping off the twigs and small branches, like after a storm in the fall when the leaves are off the trees, but every time I returned to consciousness I could see the leaves on the trees, and feel the hot and dry July air. I was groggy, and totally unaware of the passing of time.

I heard music. I looked around and couldn't see anything, then began to pass out again, but the music brought me around. It sounded like it was coming from the front of the truck. I couldn't see anything from where I was sitting.

Closing my eyes again, I could hear the music clearer. Opening my eyes, I looked behind the truck, then under it. Nothing. Then I crawled to the front of the truck. Still I couldn't see anything, so I crawled back to the right rear tire. Leaning against the tire, I could hear the music again. It sounded like it was coming through a four-inch pipe or hose into my left ear.

I began crawling again, looking for the source of the music, but couldn't find a thing. I made my way around to the left front of the truck, and managed to get up on one knee. As I looked around, the music stopped.

I was just dropping to all fours again when a movement caught my eye. Looking up the canyon, and down off the road, I saw a boy. When he saw me, he ducked out of sight. Then two heads appeared, two boys.

I tried to speak, but I don't think any sound was coming out. The wind was blowing, too, making a lot of noise. I motioned for the boys to come over to me. They ducked out of sight. I suppose they thought I was probably drunk, and with all my rolling around in the dirt, plus my unshaven face I probably didn't look very good either. I dropped back to my hands and knees and began crawling back to my place by the right rear wheel.

"Hello there. What's wrong?" someone asked. I looked up to see a man walking towards me. I waited until he was near then told him I had a terrible pain in my back and chest. I asked if I could hire him to take me home. I told him where I lived. He told me to give him a minute to explain to the other vehicle in his party what was happening. A few minutes later we were on our way down the canyon.

I looked up in the sky and quietly said, "Thank you very much." I fought desperately to stay awake, or conscious, so I could continue to give the driver directions to my home. I kept drifting into unconsciousness, but every time he had a question, I seemed to be able to rally enough to give him the answer he needed.

When we arrived home I had him pull onto my brother's lawn across the street and honk the horn. The man seemed hesitant, but did as I asked.

My brother, Clyde, came around the corner of

the house, and when he saw me, he said I had had a heart attack. That was the first time I realized what had happened to me. Clyde backed out his car and pulled me into the back seat with him while the fellow from the other car drove us to the hospital.

I stopped fighting to remain conscious. Finally, I could relax, knowing Clyde would take over. The next three or four days were blank.

I was in the hospital three weeks. During that time I kept reliving what had happened during the heart attack. Some of the events came back to me at that time, but it was early the following winter that I remembered the rest of what happened.

Sometimes I wonder why I kept going back and forth between consciousness and the other dimension, and why the tunnel with the light at the other end suddenly disappeared just as I was about to enter it. And what about that moment when the flesh was falling off my arm? How near death was I?

I can't help but wonder that maybe the power on the other side had made a mistake, and my time was not then, or they didn't have a place prepared for me.

Whatever the situation was, they solved or avoided the problem by letting me return, and I'm glad they did. So is my wife.

Ned L.

CHAPTER EIGHTEEN

LIFE IS LIKE AN AQUARIUM

On November 21, 1988, I was admitted to the local hospital with a moderately high fever, pneumonia, and severe sinus headaches. I was diagnosed as having severe sinusitis. On Thanksgiving Day, November 24, 1988, I was given a pass to leave the hospital to go home and enjoy Thanksgiving dinner with my family. It was such an exhausting and unpleasant experience due to the severity of my infection that I returned to the hospital immediately after the dinner.

The following day I went to my dentist and requested an X-ray of my teeth. My upper molars were causing me so much pain that I thought I might have to have a root canal. He took one look at the X-rays and asked me if I had a metal plate in my sinus area. The infection was so bad that it appeared my

sinuses were filled with metal. Never had he seen
such bad sinusitis. Since it had progressed so far as to
even encompass the nerves of my teeth, it was of no
surprise that I was experiencing excruciating pain.
When I returned to the hospital, I contacted Dr. Hill,
my pulmonary specialist, and told him the results. He
suggested that I have an ear, nose and throat (E.N.T.)
specialist examine me and determine the next step.

Saturday morning, November 26, Dr. Arbon, an
E.N.T., came to my room where he conducted a quick
preliminary exam of my sinuses with an eight inch
metal probe that had cotton wrapped on the end. He
carefully pushed the probe all the way up into the top
of my sinuses through my nose. Needless to say, it
was quite an uncomfortable experience. At that point,
he determined that an emergency operation was justi-
fied to relieve me of any further pain. It took three
hours to find someone at my insurance company who
was willing to give permission to operate, and it took
another two hours to pull the operating team together.

At 3:00 p.m., I was admitted to the hospital pre-
op holding room. As I was going through the pre-op
procedures, I told Dr. Arbon that I was cystic fibrotic,
and that when he opened my sinuses he would discov-
er a serious scarring problem associated with the

mucosa membranes. What would normally be an hour long operation would probably take two or three hours. He politely assured me that everything would be all right.

I was admitted into the operating room at 3:30 in the afternoon. I had a nice talk with the operating nurse who remembered me from previous surgeries. I remember thinking as the anesthesiologist started the sodium pentothal into my I.V. tube that I had only five more seconds on earth. I quickly dismissed this thought with the rationale that this was a common fear for anyone who was about to be operated on. Then I went out.

As I came out of the operating room, I remember talking to my wife, Wanda, and saying that I must not have done too well in the operation because I was not in my regular room. I remember having wires attached to me everywhere and an oxygen mask on my face. I could hear a machine beeping my heart rate, and a blood pressure cuff squeezing my arm every two minutes. Wanda explained to me that I had lost a lot of blood during the surgery, and they had put me into the Intermediate Care Unit until my vital signs were back to normal.

I was in Intermediate Care for three days. I

received 5 pints of blood. I was constantly harassed by the nurses who were telling me to be quiet and to keep my arms down. They kept telling me to relax and to leave my employees alone. I must have been hallucinating that I was at work instructing my employees.

On Tuesday November 29, I was released from Intermediate Care and I was put into a private room on the sixth floor. Dr. Arbon came into my room and removed the packing which had been tightly packed into my sinuses to prevent bleeding. It felt as though he had packed my nose with miles of pipe cleaners. As he was pulling the packing out of my sinuses through my nostrils, it seemed as if there would never be an end to the packing. The pain was excruciating. I was crying from the intense pain, but he just kept pulling and pulling. My wife told me the scene was so gruesome that my mother elected not to come into the room. She also could not bear to hear me screaming in pain. She had to walk to the opposite side of the hospital in order to escape my sounds of agony. Dad did a little better, but even he had to leave the room due to the obvious pain I was experiencing.

I remember apologizing to the doctor for being such a cry baby, that I usually handled pain better than that. I was just so exhausted from all the pain, loss of blood, and trauma, that the only way I could release my feelings was through crying. Once he was through, all I wanted was a pain shot so I could go to sleep. I was totally exhausted, both physically and emotionally.

In the early morning hours of Wednesday, November 30, I suddenly awakened to the startling realization that I had left my body and was traveling in a giant, dark tunnel or corridor towards a very bright light, brighter than any light I had ever seen. Had it not been for the fact that I had read in books and magazines about people who had died and described their experience, I might not have realized where I was until I had entered the light. As it was, I stopped traveling half way through the tunnel to get my bearings. Realizing that I was physically dead, and remembering my fears of death as a mortal, I immediately checked to see if I was dressed or not. I was quite relieved to find that I was dressed. I was in a white garment that covered me from neck to ankle and down to my wrists. The texture was of a material that I had never felt before. It was a heavy woven material that appeared to be as coarse as wool but felt as smooth as silk.

I then realized I was not feeling any sense of fear, and the transition that we call death is a very pleasant and peaceful process without any associated pain. It was at this point I realized that for the first time in my life, I was not feeling any pain anywhere in my body. I felt good and totally refreshed all over. Oh, what a great feeling! I did not want it to end.

My next thought was to check the tunnel and see how it felt. I walked over to the walls and touched them. They were somewhat rough and slightly undulating. I noticed that the tunnel was dimly lit, like that of an optometrist's examination room. It was not a stark, cold darkness but rather it was a soft, relaxing dimness. I then noticed that I was standing approximately in the middle of the total length of the tunnel.

I realized at that point that I was alone in the tunnel. I could not see anyone else. Although I knew I was alone, I did not feel alone. "Someone" was with me. I then thought to myself, "With all the hundreds of people who must have died at the very instant that I died, where are they? Perhaps they have their own tunnel and their own experience. Where are the spirit beings that are supposed to escort me to the light?" I later learned that God knew me well enough to know that I would choose to return to earth. Thus, I would not need any escorts to accompany me to the light.

As I was going through this analytical process in the tunnel, I began to notice that there was a soft and gentle "fatherly voice" talking to me. I turned 90 degrees to my left, and facing the light I slightly inclined my head to see where the "voice" was coming from. I saw no one, but I undoubtedly heard someone talking to me through my mind and not my ears. I began responding to the "voice" through my thoughts without opening my mouth. It was a pure telepathic communication which transcended communication through spoken word.

My thought at that moment was, "How can this 'voice' communicate to me through just my mind and not my ears?" I learned that it was not necessary to understand right then. I began to ask the "voice" questions: "Why am I here?"

He responded, "You are here because you have earned the right to be here based on the amount of pain you have suffered in your life. You have suffered as much in 37 years as a healthy man would have suffered in 87 years." That led me to understand that the amount of pain I suffered was the determining factor in allowing my spirit to leave its body. For me it was physical pain while perhaps for others, it may be spiritual, emotional, intellectual or social pain. Regardless of the source of pain, pain is still pain and the body suffers from it. What an interesting principle this is, and having suffered the pain I have, it certainly makes sense.

I continued with my questions: "Why did I have to suffer so much in the mortal world?"

"You chose your disease and the amount of pain that you would be willing to suffer when you were in the premortal world. It was your choice."

I then realized that in an eternal perspective, I was not a victim of my disease but rather its controller or agent due to my premortal choice. True, I cannot control the inevitable, slow deterioration of my mortal body, but I can control how I handle my illness emotionally and psychologically. I can choose to endure my suffering as a martyr immersed in self-pity with the idea that God is punishing me, or I can learn to endure it with a positive, eternal perspective knowing that God loves me and is allowing me this experience. I am only a victim of myself if I choose to be. I have the disease, it doesn't have me. It is all a matter of attitude for me.

Suddenly I realized that I had come "home." Everything I was learning and experiencing was familiar to me. There were no surprises. I compare the familiarity of where I was to that of where I grew up as a child. There is a distinguishable ambiance in the home I grew up in. You could blind fold me and take me through homes all over the world, but when I entered the home that I grew up in, I would know it. It would be familiar to me. So it was at death—I had returned "home." I recognized it after 37 years of wearing the "mortal blind fold."

Even the "voice" was familiar to me. I refer to it as the "voice" out of respect to my spiritual Father who created me. I no longer have merely a belief in God, rather, I know that He lives and I know His voice. I also know that He is a caring and loving Being with a capacity for love that transcends any love that I have ever experienced on earth. The atmosphere of love in which I was enveloped was as tangible and life-sustaining as water is to a fish. I could actually feel it. Love is the essence of God!

I then learned that everything I had experienced in my life was possible due to the love God has for me. It is by His unconditional love that He allowed me the experience of earth life replete with its trials, conse-quences, and rewards. I now realize at what risk He allowed me to experience life—the risk of my failing

to learn responsibility and accountability for everything that happens to me. This includes the lesson of
not being a victim to anything which would tempt me
to resign my accountability. And, He allowed me to
come to earth even at the risk of my choosing not to
return to Him. Out of His pure love, He has allowed
me this great but extremely short experience that we
call mortal life to choose eternal consequences or eternal rewards.

I also realized that everything that I was learning and experiencing was consistent with what religion had taught me. Again, there were no surprises.
Where others who have died may have left organized
religion, perhaps due to teachings and beliefs which
are inconsistent with the reality of the next world, I
was drawn closer to my mine.

Both the speed and the process with which I
was learning are unexplainable. I felt as though my
whole body was an antenna or receptor through which
light and knowledge were rushing in. It was as if my
whole body was filled with light. Everything was
crystal clear. My conversation and my learning
process were happening simultaneously. It was an
exhilarating experience!

I no longer have the driving need to seek for

positions in order to prove either my worthiness or my importance to myself and others. I know and have experienced something much greater than the glory of mortal men. I now realize that a position is simply an opportunity to have a greater sphere of positive influence and service to a greater number of people. I am now, more than ever before, concerned about the well being of others. I have a deep reverence and respect for all life.

With a greater understanding of God, earth life, and the next life, I was ready to continue my journey down the tunnel towards the light. At that point, I heard my three year old son, Eric, calling to me from the opposite end of the tunnel. I turned around and saw him and Jacob, my oldest son, sitting on my wife's lap. Eric asked, "Dad, what are you doing?" He did not move his lips during our conversation. Again, it was all through the mind.

I replied, "What do you mean?"

He again asked, "Dad, what are you doing?"

I answered, "I don't know. What am I doing?" I simultaneously was asking the voice the same question.

The voice then asked, "What do you want to do?"

I replied, "If I choose to go back to my family, what will be the consequences? And can I go back?"

He answered, "You may return, but you may lose your reward. There are no guarantees. You will also experience greater pain than you have ever felt in your life to this point."

I asked, "What gives me the right to go back if I choose to?" "You have learned accountability and responsibility. You have got it! If you choose to go back, you will have the responsibility to teach your family and your employees."

"My employees?" I asked with a startled voice.

"Yes, your employees," He confirmed. "But, you do have the right to go on. What is your choice?"

I remember analyzing my options, risk, and current reward. My reward was revealed to me in the tunnel. Eternal happiness was within my grasp.

"I choose to return," I answered while thinking to myself that I may live to regret my choice.

He asked me, "Are you sure?"

I replied, "Yes."

"Are you sure?" He asked again.

"Yes," I replied.

"Are you sure?" He asked for a final time.

"YES, I am sure."

I knew at that point that in order for me to return, all I had to do was turn my head back towards my family and I would return. I also had the thought that maybe the pain that He promised me would be during the process of my spirit re-entering my body.

The next thing I remember was waking up in my hospital bed completely soaked with sweat and the nurse asking me if I was all right. I replied that I was, but that I wanted Jeannette, the night nurse, to stay up with me for the rest of the night. For lack of a better excuse, I told her I was afraid of choking. I did not want to share what had happened to me with her. I was pretty confused emotionally. I knew it was not a dream that I had just experienced. I was afraid of going through the experience again, so I asked her not to let me fall asleep for the rest of the evening. She said she would help and then proceeded to get me fresh bed linens and pajamas due to the fact that those I was wearing were completely soaked with sweat.

Let me add parenthetically at this point that in January of 1989, I visited with Jeannette when she was taking care of one of my friends while he was in the hospital with bowel surgery. I asked her about her experience with me on "that night." She told me that it was one of the most frightening experiences of her nursing career. When she came into my room and saw me, she thought I was dead. My skin appeared grey and my eyes were open, looking far beyond the limit of the ceiling. When she touched me, I immediately went into a seizure which she could not control. I flopped all over the bed until I finally regained consciousness. And that is when I asked her not to leave me for the remainder of the night.

After getting my pajamas changed and my bed remade, I retired back to my bed in an almost upright, sitting position. Jeannette sat in the chair directly to the side and a little behind the bed. I could not see her unless I made the effort to lean over the side of the bed and look behind me.

I tried staying awake, but I must have dozed off. The next thing I remember was sitting up in my bed, looking behind me and seeing my upper torso still asleep, and Jeannette knitting in the corner. I thought to myself, "Oh no! Here I go again." Then I laid back down and woke up. Without moving one inch from the bed, I exclaimed to Jeannette, "You cannot just sit there and knit. You must keep me awake tonight."

She exclaimed with a voice that clearly demonstrated how surprised she was, "How do you know I am knitting?"

I replied, "I know everything that is going on in this room!"

"That's impossible" she exclaimed. "How can you know what I am doing without moving from your bed? You can't see me."

"Don't ask me how I know. Just trust me that I do."

If there was any question of the reality of my experience in the tunnel, there was no question now. I know what I saw, felt, heard, and said. I also retained a lot of what I learned. There is absolutely no question as to where I was.

I have, since that experience in November of 1988, experienced the pain that I was promised in the tunnel. It has been very severe and mostly centered in my right lung and intestinal track. Sometimes, even narcotics provide no comfort. It is at these times that I am tempted to regret my decision to return to mortality. But it is the thought that every day is an opportunity for a new earth experience with my family and employees that would have been lost forever if I had decided to go on to the light that gives me the strength to endure the pain. Every new and completed day is "frosting on the cake" for me, complete with its share of pain, but more than amply compensated with the

satisfaction that I am true to the commitment I made
with my Father in the tunnel. What a blessing life is!

I now realize that life is like an aquarium. I
have a 75-gallon freshwater aquarium in my living
room. In the tank there is a complete and distinct
world that my fish are living in. They are confined to
that world for their chosen lifetime. They are mostly
unaware of the greater worlds that exist around
them—my living room, my world, and my universe.
These are, indeed, separate worlds with separate living
conditions. However, all are just as real as the others.
Only when I decide to feed them or stand by the glass
and watch them does their awareness shift from their
tiny (by comparison) mundane environment to the
reality of a greater world outside of theirs. At these
times they also become cognizant of the fact that
there is a being that has control over their daily existence through his love and grace. As I feed them, I am
rewarded by their gratefulness for the food I give them,
and I am reminded of the food, both spiritual and
physical, that my Heavenly Father gives me. I, too, am
grateful. As I turn off the aquarium light, I notice that
they are bewildered and frightened of the darkness
that envelops them as indicated by their frantic dart-
ing about the tank. As I see the early morning light

slowly lighting their environment and see them come to life, I am reminded of how the Spirit works in my life. When I was without it in my life, I, too, was frightened of the dark and confused about the direction I should take in my life. The light of Christ brings hope, confidence, direction, and purpose to an otherwise dark existence.

As much as my fish want to believe at times that they are the only living things in existence, the reality is that there is a greater and mostly unseen world around them that sustains their very existence. So it is with earth and the rest of the universe, and so it is with mortality and immortality. It is a pity that only when the fish are hungry and recognize their dependence on a greater being that they acknowledge a greater world and a greater Being.

DeLynn